My Experience
As an Inmate
of the
Colored Orphan Asylum
New York City

By T. H. BARNES

Copyright © 2005 Douglass Barnes Crawford, Fanny Crawford, Miriam Crawford

First Edition, 2005
Second Edition, 2017

All rights reserved. No reproduction, copy or transmission of this publication may be made without written permission from the publisher.

ISBN 978-0-9991839-0-8

Proofread by: Barbara Crawford, Douglass Crawford and Fanny Crawford

Design and Layout: José Rosapepe

Cover: Scan from a copperplate of T. H. Barnes

Contact: Fanny Crawford at 301-730-1638 or fanitsky@hotmail.com

CONTENTS

My experience as an inmate of the 1
colored orphan asylum

Photos. 38-44

Fraternal 74

Frederick Douglass 75

Endnotes 79

MY EXPERIENCE AS AN INMATE OF THE COLORED ORPHAN ASYLUM NEW YORK CITY

By T. H. BARNES

I have been requested by Dr. Pitman, Superintendent of the above institution (1911-1937), to write my life and experience in said institution, which I will attempt to the best of my ability and recollection, although sixty years have elapsed since I left its portals.

In thinking over the subject, I have concluded that it would be quite necessary to state who I am, by giving a short but graphic history of my life prior to entering, and since leaving, the asylum. Trusting that the narrative will be interesting, I will begin with my parents.

My father, Henry Barnes, was born in or near Richmond, Virginia, about the year 1818 - a slave, having no definite record of his parents. When but a boy, he was bought by a wealthy resident of Hagerstown, Maryland, whose name was Barnes. This man was an Englishman by birth and a slaveholder. He would own only young black men, and each one he would cause to learn a trade (mechanical). Contrary to the laws of the state (at that time), he taught his slaves to read and write; also the first rules of Arithmetic. His business was to lease or hire out these slaves according to their trades. Their education would enable them to keep time and record of work performed and report the same to him at the conclusion of the contract.

About the year 1835 Barnes, realizing that he had grown old and infirm, called in his slaves, nineteen in number. Secretly at night he confided with them, stating that he had not long to live, and as they had served him well, he had concluded to liberate them. Handing each one their individual free papers and two hundred dollars in money, he admonished and demanded that they immediately that night go to the barn, take horses and wagons sufficient to carry them across the state line into Pennsylvania, and leave the same at a place he had designated and arranged. From there, with all haste and caution, move on to Canada. He also requested that each one take his name as their own; to which they readily and solemnly consented and agreed. Thus, then and there, nineteen young colored men took the name of Barnes.

He told them to go with all haste, as his family and heirs in the morning, learning what had been done, would take immediate steps to adjudge him insane and irresponsible, and start men and dogs in pursuit. If overtaken, they would be brought back and sold farther south. They immediately obeyed, taking an affectionate goodbye. These nineteen young men would bring at least fifteen hundred dollars apiece on the slave market, and with the money he had given them they represented the bulk of the old man's fortune.

Daybreak found the fugitives over the state line at the place designated to leave the horses. Obtaining other conveyance, they at once pushed on to Lewistown, Mifflin County, a station of the Underground Railroad. The Underground Railroad was the name of a secret organization of men and women, principally white, whose purpose and object was to secretly harbor and assist runaway slaves, en-route to Canada or a place of safety. This organization had stations all along the border states and was instrumental in rescuing hundred of Negroes from slavery. Canada was the haven. Once there, they were safe and free.

At this time the fugitive slave law was in force. The Supreme Court of the United States decreed (Judge Taney's decision) that no Negro had any rights or privileges that a white man was bound to respect. They enacted the fugitive slave law that authorized the arrest and return to former master of any runaway slaves.

At Lewistown, Pennsylvania, where the Barnes fugitives stopped for rest, their pursuers, constables and slave hunters, overtook them. Seventeen of the refugees got away toward Canada. Two were separated from their fellows, but friends secreted and hid them. They remained there several days until their pursuers had gone and the authorities of the town, recognizing and accepting their free papers as legal, made arrangements for their safety. These two were Henry Barnes (the father of the writer) and Jerry Barnes, both men having trades and able to read and write. They soon found lucrative employment and concluded to remain in Lewistown.

An interesting episode occurred that night. So close were the pursuers, that the friends of the fugitives had scarcely time to hide the two; Henry under a barn and Jerry down a deep water well, that was operated with a bucket and windlass. It was located on the edge of the street, just opposite the home of a very old spinster known as Aunt Mattie Smith, who had the unsavory reputation of being a witch. Early next morning, Aunt Mattie, not knowing what had happened the night before, went to the well for water. She cranked hard and long. Then lo and behold, what came up with the bucket? A black man! Seeing the apparition, she dropped the handle. Down went Jerry to the bottom of the well and Mattie, thoroughly frightened, ran into the house screaming at the top of her voice. "My God, my God, the devil in the well." A man close by, hearing her cries, suspected the truth. He called down to Jerry to lay quiet, not to come up 'til night when he would be taken out. Then going into the house, he consoled Aunt Mattie, telling her she was dreaming and that he would draw the water. So doing, Jerry was taken out of the well that night more dead than alive, after twenty-four or more hours standing in the cold water. He was restored to normal and lived many years as a useful and prosperous citizen.

Henry Barnes was a man about five feet four inches high, weight one hundred and sixty pounds, had a dark complexion, was quick in movement, athletic, had a genial disposition, and was strictly religious of the Wellsley Methodist type. He was a seed man, landscape gardener, as per record of 1840. He married Jane Williams, a girl of eighteen, bright Mulatto, five feet six inches in height, of robust health and physique, but meager education. Her parents were free born sturdy Pennsylvania farmers. Her father, tall in stature, copper color, of Negro, Indian and Dutch blood, died at the age of ninety-four. Her mother, short in stature, white, of Dutch blood, died at ninety-two.

A description of my mother's people would be interesting and unique. My grandmother was one of three sisters, Sarah, Polley and Mary Couper of Cooperstown, Pennsylvania. Each one married colored men (Mulattos) - Daniel Williams, Samuel Molson, and Samuel Greenly. To each family was born sixteen children. My grandparents were Daniel and Sarah Williams. My parents were Henry and Jane Barnes. To them were born five children - Martha, Mary, James, Thomas and Peter, the first three dying under ten years.

I, Thomas Henry Barnes, was born January 2, 1849 in Lewistown, Pa.; my brother was born two years later.

My father died in 1857 of pneumonia (quick consumption they called it). He had been a very hard working man and a good provider. He owned his own home with three acres of land on which he cultivated and raised garden, herb and flower seeds. He was scrupulously neat in dress; good manners were his hobby. He was an active leader in church work. My mother vied with him in neatness and enjoyed the reputation of being the best cook and housekeeper in the town. I distinctly remember every detail of our home life, and I am proud to relate that it was ideal, strictly conforming to the religious observance of the Methodist creed. My mother's education and schooling were very limited, but she was a natural mathematician and had wonderful memory of names, dates, and details. She was enthusiastic on the subjects of education, politics and temperance; was well posted on all the great national questions of the time. It was she who gave me my first lesson in politics, making me a perpetual Republican.

I have a very vivid recollection of the events leading up to the Civil War - the formation of the Republican Party by the Whigs, Abolitionists, and Free Soil Democrats, nicknamed the "Wideawakes." This fusion nominated Millard Filmore, Republican candidate for President in 1856, with James Buchanan, Democratic candidate, representing the Southern slave holding element.

Just across the road from where we lived was a great field used for public purposes, campus parade ground. The local military company under Colonel Eisenbise, the Logan Guards, came to drill and sham battle. Barbecues were held, political meetings, etc. Young as I was, I saw and heard much that deeply interested me; my mother took pains to teach and explain the different events.

To illustrate, I will relate an incident of the time of a political campaign. A procession was coming, brass band, flags, banners, etc. She called me, lifted me up on the fence, told me to take off my hat, throw it in the air, hurrah, and make a joyful noise as loud as possible as they passed, for these men were Republicans. They were in favor of freedom and schools for our people. The passing procession returned our salute. Mother and I received an enthusiastic ovation, besides a lot of big copper cents that were thrown to me. A few days later another similar procession appeared. Mother grabbed brother and I by the arms, forced us into the house, locked the door, and put down the curtains. All colored people in the neighborhood did the same. The procession passed. We received an ovation - yes, but with derisive epithets, and a shower of stones. Mother explained that these men represented the southern slave holding democracy, then in power of the government.

I didn't intend to write a political history, but simply to give an outline of the fundamental principles that brought about the war of the rebellion and caused the most disgraceful tragedy and massacre in the history of the United States. The July Riots of 1863 caused the murder of hundreds of colored people and the burning of the Colored Orphan Asylum, wherein Jefferson Davis, Robert Tombs, Valandingham, Beauregard, and Lee were the prime arch traitors to their country. Such names as Abraham Lincoln, John Brown, Charles Sumner, Harriet Beecher Stowe, William Lloyd Garrison, Wendell Phillips and Fred Douglass were abolitionists of slavery and the preservation of the Union.

Mother was proud to acquiesce of father's attainments, as it was rare, very rare, in those days for colored men to have book education.

I am writing this narrative on a portable folding desk, made of mahogany, twenty inches long by ten inches square, with drawer and compartment for stationery. This desk was given to my father by his former master. It is lined with a newspaper dated 1825. Also lying before me is my father's family Bible, dated 1814. After his death, mother, brother and I went to live with my grandparents. I was sent to school, as it was called. Set apart, exclusive for colored children; crude and primitive in the extreme. A correct description of the building, equipment, teacher and pupils should be written, engraved, and placed in the state archives at Harrisburg, Capitol, as an educational curiosity. The funny pictures in our Sunday papers cannot equal it.

My mother died early in the spring of 1860. Although seventy-nine years have passed, the incidents of her sickness and death are as vivid as though but yesterday. She had been sick about two years. Time and space will not permit detail of the saddest event of my life, but I cannot refrain from giving the principal event, her death. The last month, supposing that she was improving, we left home on a Saturday afternoon, Mother, brother and I, in a carriage to visit friends in the country about three miles distant. That evening she ate a hearty supper and was joyous and happy. In the morning about daybreak she called me from an adjoining room to her bedside. Leaning over, putting her arm around me, placing our home keys in my hand, she gave me explicit and minute directions as to the care of her personal effects, money, jewelry, etc.

She was perfectly rational and cool. Drawing me closer to her as she lay in bed, she said, "Now Tommy, always be a good boy as I have taught you. Take good care of your brother Peter." She kissed me on the forehead and bade me back to bed. I had turned to pass through the door; I looked back. She had drawn herself upon the bed, placing her hands upon her breast. I saw her gasp, went quickly to her, called her, took her hand in mine, but she was dead. Oh, what a moment! I cannot express my feelings! Brother was asleep. I was in the house alone. The people had gone to the barn to do the milking. I called them. They could not believe her dead. I immediately started for home, walked the three miles, followed her instructions minutely. In her room I sat down and in anguish cried aloud, but there was no one to hear me. I fully realized my plight. Mother dead, I was an orphan. I took courage, something seemed to say to me, "Be a little man." I went out, locked the door, and went my way back to the country house. They had telegraphed to my Uncle, my mother's brother, Peter A. Williams of Brooklyn, N.Y. In due time he came and conducted the funeral. When they lowered my mother in the grave, dropped those clods on the coffin - the sound - Oh, God, how horrible! I will never forget the pang; what a miserable, heartrending custom. They have done away with it and saved much heartache.

Uncle settled all the business remaining and took Grandfather (his father), brother, and I with him to Brooklyn. He was a man of ample means. He was one grand man and his wife, Aunt Caroline, an angel. They gave brother and I every attention. No pains were spared to make us comfortable and alleviate our bereavement.

My Uncle's family consisted of four persons - himself, wife, and two daughters, Elizabeth, fifteen, and Sarah, twelve. With Grandfather, brother and I there were seven. My cousins were very fair in complexion and attended white school. There was no school in that section of Brooklyn that would admit colored children. Over the river in New York was the nearest one. So Aunt, after consulting Dr. McCune Smith, the Colored Orphan Asylum physician, concluded to put us boys in that institution. Arrangements were made, and we entered that Home in the spring of 1860 as half orphans, meaning as per rules, that half orphans should pay one dollar and fifty cents per week, thus giving guardians permission to take us out at will. Full orphans paid nothing but were supposed to remain until they were thirteen or fourteen years of age, when they would be indentured or bound out to reputable persons. Farmers preferred, until they were of age, girls eighteen and boys twenty-one. At the expiration of time to receive a stipend or sum of money, girls fifty dollars and boys one hundred dollars.

How vividly do I remember our entrance to the new home in company with Aunt and Uncle. We were graciously and cordially received, all formalities necessary arranged. We were shown through the building. What a sight to us! Between two and three hundred colored boys and girls, plain, neat, and well dressed, all alike, with smiling faces were waiting, eager to meet and know the "new boys".

I will attempt to describe the building and inmates. It was a four-story brick building, including basement and attic, over and under the whole; occupying the block between 43rd and 44th streets on 5th Avenue. The architecture was old colonial, minus the columns or pillars; fully equipped with modern conveniences to date. There was hot and cold water on every floor and thorough ventilation. In the basement were spacious play rooms for boys and girls separate, bathrooms with eight large tubs, twice the ordinary size, two plunge baths, and swimming pools. The coal bins were large enough to hold a year's supply. The laundry was steam equipped with washers, wringers, mangles, and drying room. There was a storeroom and cold room for all eatables, then the boiler and engine room and also the shoe shop.

On the first floor were the main entrance, superintendent's office, director's room, and visitor's parlor, with a spacious hall running full length of the building. There was a large glass showcase displaying fancy needlework and other products of the inmates and a large black walnut box for visitor's contributions in the hall. There were children and attendant dining rooms, kitchen, pantry, infant's department and a room for manufacturing and storing clothing.

The second floor consisted of three large schoolrooms, capacity of sixty each, with adjoining classrooms and a school supplies room.

On the third floor were six large dormitories for children,

teachers, and help with sleeping rooms, bedrooms, and wardrobe. In the attic were a dormitory, store rooms, and sleeping rooms. At each end of the building and in the center were three wide stairways and fire escapes. In fact, the whole building was splendidly adapted and was well equipped, making an ideal home.

Management and Officers..... 1860

Elizabeth Bowne	Mrs. I.N. Phelps
Ellen Burling	Fanny Paxson
Hannah W. Collins	Eliza B. Stewart
Mrs. J.M. Cockroft	Mrs. J. Stokes
Mrs. S.N. Dodge	Mrs. C. Schaffer
Mary K. Day	Anna C. Tatum
Mrs. Amos R. Eno	Sarah F. Underhill
Mary Few	Lydia G. Underhill
Mrs. James Hurd	Cornelia L. Westerlo
Mrs. Caroline Hull	Mrs. E. P. Willets
Mrs. Sarah Lankford	Mrs. Rachel Whitehead
Sarah S. Murray	Anna F. Willis
Mrs. J. J. Phelps	

Mrs. M. A. Mason	1st Directress
Mrs. C. N. S. Roosevelt	2nd Directress
Mrs. A. H. Showell	Secretary
Mrs. D. W. James	Treasurer

House Staff

William E. Davis	Superintendent
Jane McClelland	Matron
Mrs. Robinson	Matron of Hospital
Benjamin Griffin	Assistant Superintendent
Mrs. Howarth	Assistant Matron

Physician

Dr. J. McCune Smith

Teachers

Mary Young	Sarah Hill
Rosalie Davis	Sarah Valentine
Eleanor McClelland	Sarah Robinson

The management consisted of a superintendent, W. E. Davis, a typical Englishman, splendidly adapted, efficient, a genial disciplinarian, and Christian gentleman - loved and respected. The matron, Miss Jane McClellan, an Irish lady, was efficient, thorough, feared and respected by all. The Assistant Superintendent, Mr. Benjamin Griffin, a colored man having special care of the boys, was all that could be asked, a wonderful, stout, strong, happy dispositioned man with discipline his hobby. Yet he made himself one of the boys. We all loved and had to obey him. He was a fine musician and had a good bass voice. His violin cello and vocal solos made us many a happy hour. The Assistant Matron, Mrs. Howard, a colored woman, having full charge of the girls, was tall, angular, well educated, scrupulously neat in dress, boasted of culture and refinement. She strictly disciplined the girls; her motto was, "Spare the rod you spoil the child." She was an ideal person for the position.

The principal teacher and superintendent of schools, Miss Mary A. Young, a Quakeress, fully conforming to the Quaker idea of dress and deportment, was a scholar, a student, an encyclopedia of knowledge and was all kindness and patience, yet firm. I was especially in her favor, and Tommy Barnes owes much to Miss Young. Her assistant in Number 1 school of sixty pupils, the oldest children, was Miss Rosey Davis, daughter of the Superintendent. She was handsome personally, brunette in complexion, short in stature with a very genial disposition, good musician and had a splendid soprano voice. She supervised the singing. She loved us because we loved music and could sing. I can see her now, waving her baton, compiling time and rhythm. Oh, how proud she was displaying us to visitors and in musical contests, when we would visit other schools or churches. We always carted off the laurels. Miss Davis tutored many a songbird in that institution, thrilled with delight hundreds of people, and gave the singers an accomplishment that would carry success through life. I must mention a few girls with exceptional voices, although there were many - Josephine Clark, Sarah Spencer, Fannie Wright, and Josephine Osen. Among the boys with good voices there were numbers. She had no trouble to fill parts, and Rosey Davis knew how and delighted in it. We often received invitations to Sunday School conventions and musical entertainment outside. I could relate many interesting and amusing episodes, always carrying off the palms. Our repertoire was endless, our pep and energy boundless.

   I will relate an embarrassing but amusing incident that happened at one of our exhibitions in Cooper Institute, then the largest and most popular assembly hall in the city. We were booked for a benefit entertainment, the program to consist of song, recitations and dialogues. The house was crowded, a select audience, to hear the Colored Orphans. The actors or participants, about twenty-five in number, were arranged on the stage behind an immense curtain, under the management of Miss Young and Miss Davis. The number in question was a dialogue entitled "Interrupted Speakers." The performers were four boys - Barnes, Doran, Allen and Dutton. The scheme was the first speaker comes on the stage, attempting to deliver an oration, when number two rushed onto the scene to interrupt number one while speaking, then number three interrupted number two, and number four interrupted number three. Each speaker had a speech of his own, impersonating the original. In this case, when the program number was called, Barnes stopped forward to the front of the stage and began, "My name is Normal on the Grampton Hills, my father feeds his flocks" etc *(see endnote page 79)*. Then he was to be interrupted by Doran with "I have come to bury Caesar not to praise him" etc. But Doran, looking out, saw that great throng of expectant faces, took violent stage fright and would not go, would not budge. The managers pleaded, implored, without effect, at once resorted to force, but Doran, being a stout young lad, concluded that it would be a fight to the finish, and there was some scrap. The teachers being vanquished, the other speakers reluctantly came out, all this time Barnes stood there before that host repeating over and over, "My name is Normal on the Grampton Hills, my father feeds his flocks…" for that is all he had learned of the piece. The audience, hearing the noise and confusion behind the curtain and Barnes repeating, concluding that it was all in the play, encored and encored, but their wants could not be answered; there could be no repetition. The balance of the program was a success. There are now only two, known living, who participated in that event - John A. Doran of 52 West 8th St., New York City and Thomas H. Barnes of Olean, New York.

Room Number 2 (what we called the middle school) was presided over by Miss Ellen McClelland (sister of the Matron), a stout lady noted for her dignity of manner, a good teacher, very precise, especially interested in the girls. She was assisted by Miss Lyzie Hill, a young colored woman, who had formerly been an inmate of the asylum and at the age of fourteen had been taken out and educated in a private school and returned to the institution as a teacher. She was a good one, prepossessing, loved her work and was the social leader among the older boys and girls. We had a secret organization called the Reynolds Family. Miss Lyzie was our president. Each member had a fictitious name. We numbered about twenty. Only those were admitted to the circle who were known to be positively trustworthy to keep the secret profound. Miss Lyzie's private room was our meeting place, and many a happy hour was spent with good things to eat and innocent games. She delighted in teaching the boys gallantry and the girls manners and etiquette of good society. It was all right but not in accordance with Asylum rules. We had some funny, thrilling episodes to escape detection. Miss Lyzie was our idol.

The infant or primary school was conducted by two teachers. They changed so often that I will not attempt to describe any particular one. The children's dining room was presided over by Mrs. Walker, a typical Scotch woman, short and stout, pleasant, kind and affectionate. She was neatness personified in person and work. The dining room was always perfectly clean. She delighted in telling us legends of her Scotland, calling us lads and lasses in her Scotch dialect which endeared her to us. The teachers had a private dining room, two or more of the older girls in charge.

The kitchen was large, fully equipped, and up to date, all foods cooked by steam. The cooks, then as now, were often changing.

The laundry was modern to date, presided over by two genuine Irish women, Martha and Mary Stogdale, who had been in the place a long time and had grown old but were efficient. They always wanted assistants, older boys and girls to work with their wit. We had a good time with them.

Dormitories and bedding were in charge of Miss Kate Ryan, a young Irish woman, American born, quite a different type from Martha and Mary. She was good looking, good natured, and sociable. It was a rule that the older children made their own beds each morning (two in each). Miss Ryan would inspect every bed; they had to be perfectly made and in perfect order and clean. She was very thorough; sanitation and ventilation were paramount with her. She gave us many thrills; ten below zero made no difference, fresh air she would have, every morning.

In the attic or top floor there was a dormitory for boys, also a prison or lockup for incorrigibles, as we had them occasionally.

The infant nursery was in charge of Mrs. Butler, a colored woman. She was one splendid person, so well adapted, motherly, patient, cheerful and loving. She always had a couple dozen youngsters to care for, often young babies.

The hospital, a three-story building on 44th St., was separated from the main building, yet connected by enclosed passageways. It was perfectly equipped with hospital pertinence including a school for convalescents. Mrs. Penton and Mrs. Carter were the principal nurses. No amount of praise would do these women justice. They were Christian, proficient and professional. I speak from personal experience under their care. Dr. McCune Smith was the attending physician, an eminent practitioner, standing second to none among the doctors of the city. He was a member of the Board of Health. I knew him personally, as a personal friend of the family (my Uncle). His assistant was a young M.D., Dr. Dunbar; their office was at 55 West Broadway.

Dr. McCune Smith

Dr. McCune Smith was a colored man of medium height and rather corpulent; had a fine head, lofty brow, quick dazzling eyes. He was a distinguished graduate of the University of Glasgow, an accomplished writer, fluent speaker and a member of the Board of Health. He was an authority on questions of hygiene and sanitation. His knowledge of history, literature and science made him a powerful exponent of the race question as an abolitionist.

I must relate an incident to illustrate one of Dr. Smith's methods. During the winter of '61 and '62 I had an attack of sore throat and was sent to the hospital but soon recovered. There was a school for convalescents in the hospital, presided over by a Miss Robinson, a young colored woman. She was a very pleasant and agreeable teacher. The school curriculum was simple, consisting principally of story reading by the teacher and drawing pictures on the black board by the pupils, all of which I enjoyed immensely. The doctor, in making his rounds, pronounced me well and ordered me back to regular school. I protested, stating that I was not well. The doctor very curtly replied to the nurse, "Give Thomas a dose of cod liver oil every night and morning. Perhaps he will prefer that to school." I took the oil. It was not Scott's Emulsion, tasteless, odorless, given with sugar or something nice. It was the old fat, thick, crude cod liver oil, administered with a big iron spoon with a short handle, deep, narrow bowl and a sharp wedge-shaped point made to pry open the patient's mouth to force the dose. About the time the second dose was administered, I concluded I was well and went back to school.

By his advice I was sent to the institution. All through my stay he gave brother and I special attention in regard to our health. After four years, it was my duty and pleasure to carry him with horse and buggy to and from the Hudson River Railroad Station at 152nd Street. The last visit he made to the Asylum he had become old, infirm and retired from practice.

The daily routine for the children was exacting and thorough. At 5:00 a.m. a bell rang, all were up, beds made, toilet arranged, and at 6:30 assembled in the dining room for Bible reading and prayer. There were fifteen minutes for breakfast, bread and milk, quality the best and quantity sufficient. In winter, chocolate, cocoa, or cereals were served. We played until 8:30, school at 9:00. It was opened with prayer and singing; recess at 10:45 and out at 12:00 for dinner at 12:30. Each day there was a change of fare - soup, stew, fish, and roast. Friday, visitor's day, we had a full roast beef dinner. School began at 1:00, with recess during the afternoon, and lasted until 4:00. Supper was served at 6:00 and alternated mush and milk, rice and cereals, etc. Each session opened and closed with song and prayer. We were sent to bed at 8:00 in winter and 9:00 in summer, marching in single file with perfect order to and from meals, school and bed. On Saturday there was a half holiday.

On Sunday the whole building was under the management of one teacher, alternating. There was strict religious observance of the day. Cold meals were served and there were no playthings. School room Number 2 was always used for assembly meetings. Sunday School was conducted by teachers from outside; frequently some pastor or layman would give a sermon or talk in the afternoon. Weather permitting, a few would be selected to answer invitations from some outside Sunday School.

Mr. Chapman, Missionary

Of the many Christian women and men that came to us from outside to teach Sunday School, I must specially mention a Mr. Chapman, a young man of twenty-five or thirty years, representing one of the downtown churches. He was ideal, not only in Sunday School but would come down in the play rooms and make himself one of us. Finally he was requested and accepted as a missionary to India.

Our farewell meeting was a sad one. Miss Rose Davis composed and set to music a special piece for the occasion. We sang with so much feeling that he completely broke down, as many of us did. I can remember the chorus:

Farewell, farewell loved one, farewell,
A lingering, fond farewell.
We will miss you in our meeting on the Holy Sabbath Day,
Miss your warm and friendly greeting,
Miss you as we sing and pray.
For across the wide spread waters
Over dashing waves and foam,
'Mid far India's sons and daughters
Soon will be your mission home.
Farewell, loved one, farewell,
A lingering, fond farewell.

He went but returned in about two years, broken in health. He made several visits; taught us a Brahma dialect hymn, much of which I remember, but cannot produce in writing for fear you will think me swearing.

A unique feature of Sunday evening was the distribution of a specially prepared cake we called a Boliver. The dimensions were about five inches across, one-inch thick, with round, scalloped edges. The composition was not patented or copyrighted, but no infringement was ever known. The ingredients, unlimited in variety, were flour, molasses, raisins, citron, figs, berries, dates, nuts, or any dried fruit, all mixed with some ingredient that made the cake insoluble and indestructible. We used them as a medium of exchange, receivable for all debts - one or more Bolivers for a top, ball, knife, etc. They were also often used as a weapon of combat. I have known the Shylocks to have a half dozen or more in possession from one week to the next, yet the Boliver, all things to the contrary, when masticated, was palatable, good eating, and digestible.

Holidays were rigidly observed. On the Fourth of July, patriotism ran high. Having saved our money for the occasion, we spent all for crackers, powder, etc. In the evening we were allowed to go on the housetop to observe private and municipal fireworks. The next day a boy that could not show a burn or scar was considered a traitor to his country. Thanksgiving and Christmas were the astronomical events of the year. Not one of the old school could ever forget those days - living in the greatest expectation for days before. Then as our own wagon came down from town laden with candies from "Ridley's" and other good things from Acker-Merril Co, the expressmen bringing loads of sweetmeats and groceries from other dealers, the two-wheeled butcher carts running in, loaded down with turkey, chicken, duck and geese, our spirits rose still higher. In the morning those splendid carriages came to the front door, those grand ladies with their liveried attendants bringing in packages, bundles, and boxes of toys, beautiful books, and holiday goods in great profusion. The distribution in the school and the playrooms brought happiness to the donors and gladness, joy and gratitude to the children. The services in the assembly room were expressive of the spirit of the day by prayer and songs of thanksgiving. Were we thankful? Were we grateful? God knew we were. Words cannot express our appreciation. The chorus of one of our Thanksgiving anthems comes to me. "He hath not dealt so with any nation, and as for his goodness, He hath not known them"...Then praise the Lord, praise the Lord with thanksgiving and song, etc. Now a verse of a Christmas carol:

> Christmas bells are ringing, ringing o'er the land,
> Triumphantly, children's voices singing, singing,
> Sound a joyous jubilee.
> 'Tis the priceless pearl we hail,
> Sent us by a father's hand.
> The Lord of life to Thee we bow,
> And thank Thee for Thy gift.

Then again for a New Year's song which comes to my mind:

> Oh where are the sweet birds that sleep in earth's bosom,
> And the songbirds gave truant shall return once again.
> Then welcome thrice welcome through happy New Year,
> Though bring us no blossoms we bid Thee good cheer.

The dinner, the banquet, the feast - how can I describe it? I cannot. The tables were covered with snow white linen, laden - yes, groaning - under the weight of everything that pertains to a Thanksgiving or Christmas banquet - roast turkey and other fowls, cooked in a manner that later day cooks know not the art. There were Irish potatoes, mashed, sweet potatoes, corn, tomatoes, celery, pickles, cranberries, oranges, and grapes; then apple, pumpkin and mince pie; everything else, nothing excepted. The teeth and appetites that only colored youngsters possess could do the occasion justice. Balthazar's feast was only an afternoon tea in comparison. Fortunate for brother and I, coming as we did from a remote country town in Pennsylvania, our mannerisms and deportment displayed a personality quite different from the city urchins and at once grafted us into the good graces of the managers. Their endearment and respect was no small asset to our contentment and well being. I was soon made a monitor or errand boy that gave me exceptional privileges. My brother, two years younger, having an impediment in his speech that hampered his advancement in school, was placed in the primary department. I, wishing to be with him, feigned ignorance and was placed in the department with him but could not long continue the deception. So, to the teacher's perplexity, and my amusement, I was moved from one class to another until in less than two weeks I was halted in Miss Young's classroom, No. 1, with pupils much older than I. It was the educational policy of the institution to teach the advanced pupils the primary or fundamental rules of the different technical studies so that after leaving the asylum, if they wished to take up any of those branches, they would know the elementary principles.

Our schoolrooms were well equipped with modern furniture; the walls covered with maps, charts, globes, and other apparatus pertaining to a grammar school. It was presided over by competent Christian teachers, devoted to their duty of giving every child the fundamental or rudiments of a Christian education. The playgrounds and rooms were large, roomy, and excellently adapted. The whole institution was complete in every particular for those times, making an ideal home for orphan children.

Such was it on the morning of July 13, 1863. President Lincoln found it absolutely necessary for more troops to carry on the war. He called on New York to fill her quota of men. Since volunteers were not available, a conscript or draft method was adopted. An organization, secession sympathizers called "Copper Heads" determined to suppress the draft, organized a mob riot, about three thousand strong, armed with all manner of weapons - guns, pistols, clubs, etc. They marched on the provost marshal's office (the place where the draft was to be held) at 47th Street and 4th Avenue about ten o'clock Monday morning July 13, 1863. The mob completely destroyed the building by fire, killing the marshal and clerk. The police and firemen fought bravely but were outnumbered and severely beaten back by the mob. Many of the police and firemen were fearfully and mortally wounded. About this time a company of the 7th regiment, 100 strong, came double quick up the avenue, halting at 46th Street. The Captain, addressing the mob, stated that he would give them 15 minutes to disperse. They defied him. When the time expired, he gave orders to fire on the mob. The excitement begs description. The soldiers had fired blank cartridges. The mob, seeing that no one was hurt, turned on the soldiers, beating them without mercy, taking away their arms, compelling retreat in the wildest manner. The captain was killed. The mob, becoming more frenzied by success, surged down the avenue to Bulls Head Hotel on the corner of 44th Street, the political headquarters for government officers. They pillaged the building then burned it.

    During this time, the mob leaders had concluded to burn the Colored Orphan Asylum, one block away. A man in the crowd, learning their design, came to the institution and notified Superintendent Davis. He could not conceive such an act possible but gave orders that all inmates should assemble in Room No. 2 for consultation and prayer. While there, the girl at the front door gave the alarm that the mob was at the front gates coming in. At this alarm, I, along with my brother and another boy and two girls, five in all, rushed down the back stairs, out through the playgrounds, and over a stone wall on 44th Street. As we were scaling the wall, an Irish man by the name of Clancy, a member of the fire department who lived just across the street, which was crowded with an excited throng of men and women, came toward us with a large club which he was carrying. He raised his arms and cried in a loud voice, "For God's sake, is there a man here that will help and protect these children?" Several responded by making a way for us through the crowd. We ran toward 6th Avenue. It was my intention to make for home, Brooklyn. The other four were clinging to me for I knew the way. We ran as fast as possible. We could not turn at 6th Avenue on account of the great crowds. Men were engaged in breaking down telegraph poles and cutting the wires. Running to the next corner, we met two ladies who knew us, had been our Sunday School teachers. We told them what had happened. They were horror stricken. One of them knelt down on the sidewalk and prayed aloud to God for our safety and the institution. They led us toward a church on 41st Street, but we were stopped and advised to go in another direction. We could see a colored man hanging from a lamppost. Fearing the same fate, we ran toward 8th Avenue. There we were escorted by three men, a policeman and two firemen, who forcibly pushed us through the crowd to the 35th Street station house (police). There we found all the inmates of the asylum. They had orderly marched out the back gates of the asylum and were escorted to safety by police and friends to the station house, a most remarkable performance, for the mob was hunting and running down all the colored people they could find. When the five of us entered the station house, everybody was dumbstruck and rejoiced for they feared we had been killed. Mr. Davis and Mr. Griffin, along with practically all the attendants, were in the station. Many of the teachers were taken to places of safety that night.

The escape from the building was most remarkable, order was maintained, marching out by twos; policemen, firemen, and citizens protected the procession. Many graphic and exciting incidents occurred. One little girl, after getting out on the street, rushed back into the building and secured a large Bible, which was about all she could carry, and made her escape unmolested. Mrs. Carter, a nurse in the hospital, with a child in each arm was kicked and knocked downstairs, but providentially was not seriously hurt.

The building was sacked, robbed, and burned to the ground. Fiends in the shape of human beings pillaged with savage delight. O'Brien, chief of the fire department, was killed on the front steps in his attempt to prevent the mob from entering the building. Many tragic acts were enacted. A full and correct description has not been written. The police bravely defended the station house. Many colored people had been brought there for refuge and several hundred crowded into a building intended for thirty-five men. Windows and doors were barred with iron bedsteads. During the first three nights and days the mob made many attempts to enter the building but were beaten back. They tried to fire the place by barrels of oil against the side. The horror of those days and nights cannot be described. In the basement were ten small cells, five on either side of a hall, intended for one prisoner each. There were stone floors and walls, water faucet and sink, stationary basin, and a rough plank bunk with grated doors. We were crowded into this basement. There was only standing room. We could not lie or sit down. The weather was extremely hot, and there was no ventilation except through the back door that opened into a small yard to which we were forbidden on account of attracting attention. Many times we made frantic rushes into this yard when the mob tried to gain entrance into the front. Had they gained entrance we would have been massacred or burned to death.

On Tuesday morning the police began to bring in prisoners, and we were compelled to vacate the cells. A consumptive boy lay under a bench in the cell where two burley, drunken prisoners were put; the boy had been overlooked. When his friends discovered him the two men had beat and kicked him insensible before we could get the police to rescue him. Other prisoners would strike at us through the bars of the doors. They would let the water run on the floor, compelling us to stand in the filthy water from their cells. It was nearly twenty-four hours before we got anything to eat. The first bread came by a German woman disguised as a rioter. She was arrested, brought in with loaves of bread secreted in her clothing. Unloading, she passed out through the back door, over a fence, through the basement of a house on the next street. This she repeated many times, later bringing meat and other eatables. This was a heroic act. Had she been discovered by the mob it would have cost her life. Thus we lived for eighty hours, until Thursday the 16th, when the first regiment of soldiers, veterans from the Gettysburg fight, put in an appearance. They were Zouaves, a type of soldier peculiar to the Civil War. These soldiers escorted us with other refugees from the 7th Avenue Arsenal to a gun boat lying in the North River and carried us to Blackwell's Island in the East River.

I should have stated that the bitter hatred to President Lincoln and opposition to the draft was well known to the city authorities. Mayor Opdike, a noble and loyal man, fearing and expecting an outbreak, called on Governor Seymore at Albany for troops or assistance to defend the city. Governor Seymore, being a southern sympathizer, declined to give help, stating that the city should take care of itself. The city was helpless except for the police. They were indignant. All available troops had been sent to Gettysburg to prevent the rebels from invading Pennsylvania. The mob leaders, knowing the sentiment or attitude of the Governor and the unprotected condition of the city, took this advantage and for a week waged a most horrible riot of pillage, fire and murder. Churches, schoolhouses, public buildings, and private homes fell under their hands. Every house known to contain a colored man or a Republican was secretly marked with red chalk for destruction. Hundreds of colored men were hung on lampposts or killed otherwise. Many were run into the river and drowned. All communication was cut off. Telegraph wires were cut, railroad tracks torn up, and ferry boats sunk or disabled. All possible escape from the city was cut off. Hundreds of colored people hid on housetops, in cellars, woods and graveyards. Children and adults were found dead in their hiding places.

Blackwell's Island contained the penal and charity institutions of the city - penitentiary, alms house, workhouse, and lunatic asylum. We were domiciled in the alms house, one of four large stone buildings three stories high and a hundred or more feet long.

Thursday the 16th, when we were told that soldiers had come to escort us to a boat, our joy and fear knew no bounds. Joy to know that we were getting out of a horrible place and fear that the soldiers could not cope with the mob and a repetition of Monday's tragedy, when the soldiers were beat down, lurked in our hearts. But these were real soldiers, trained by actual service in battle, begrimed by exposure, resolute and determined by discipline, about a thousand strong. They were arranged in single file on either side of the front entrance of the station house out into and down the street, with guns and bayonet at charge. The officer in command, standing high on the steps, in a loud voice to the crowd, demanded the crowd to disperse at once, telling them that at the slightest disturbance or malicious act they would be fired upon and without reserve. Then we marched out by twos, between the lines of soldiers. Oh, what a thrill, coming out into the fresh air, seeing those bronzed and begrimed regulars, the street crowded with rioters, men and women, half clothed, half naked, looking like fiends, armed with all manner of weapons, ready to commit any crime. We expected grave trouble but instead there was a lull, a silence. The mob was in awe of the determined aspect of those soldiers. We were escorted to the North River, and there we boarded the police boat or gunboat. All that could be were put down in the hull of the vessel, others in the cabins or out of sight. The decks were cleared for action, with several field pieces (small cannon) and men armed for action. Thus we proceeded at a very slow speed around Manhattan to Blackwell's Island. Every precaution was taken not to attract attention for fear that boats would put out from shore to sink us. This again was great suspense until we landed safely at the pier on the Island.

There at the Island was another scene. Because the weather was excessively hot, the hundreds that were crowded in that boat for nearly two hours were nearly suffocated. Many women and children had to be carried ashore, laid on the dock and restoratives used to bring them to normal. At the alms house we received a bountiful supply of food and refreshment. Completely exhausted from fear and privation, we lay down on the floor or anywhere. There were not beds enough for one twentieth, nor did we care. We were the first cargo of refugees to land. That night other boatloads were brought, and the refugees crowded in. Such a sight! I cannot describe it. In that great building of three floors, large wide balconies on each side and end, wide iron stairways three on a side, at night every available inch was taken. Every step was occupied. In a few days there were over two thousand fugitives on the island. The cries and lamentations of those people were heartrending. Few families, if any, were whole. They had been driven from their homes in the wildest fright and confusion. Their buildings were burned, the men killed or dying in hiding places. Mothers were looking for their children separated from them, children were crying for their parents.

Practically every section of the city where colored people resided had been pillaged and burned. The people, taking refuge in the Arsenal on 7th Avenue or the station houses until sent to the island, were more naked than clothed as they had no chance to secure clothing and were glad to get away with their lives. Many colored women were caught in the street, stripped of their clothes and beaten. Our children were so quickly and unexpectedly turned out that the boys had nothing on but pants and shirts, not hats or shoes. A few of the older girls had shoes. I had bought a hat from a boy on the street for three cents so was the only one to have one. The weather, being exceedingly hot with no rain, was favorable to us.

Scarcely had we arrived at the island before a new terror threatened us. We heard that the mob was organizing to cross the river to the island. We saw boats being collected for the purpose, but the police foiled the plan. Then the prisoners in the penitentiary, several hundred in number, took advantage of the situation and attempted mutiny. The officers adopted the strictest discipline, and arms were distributed and attendants ordered to shoot the first and all for disobedience.

The warden of the island, Mr. Anderson, was an ex-Army officer and a very kind and gracious man. He furnished an abundance of good food, clothing, medicine and other needs and also gave strict attention to our safety. For days we expected an attack from the mob. Loaded cannons were placed along the river front and manned, with orders to shoot the first suspicious boat. Our assistant warden, Mr. Simson, in charge of the alms house, was especially gracious to the asylum children. Each day he took squads of boys to work as we pleased or wished in the bakery, laundry, or cook house; he gave us carts to haul provisions to the different buildings on the island, and during the two months we remained, he made life happy for us. I could relate many amusing incidents that occurred. On the other hand, he was cruel in the extreme to the paupers and men under him, but to us he was very kind and generous. He always carried a brace of revolvers and a whip in his zzperience, hairbreadth escapes, etc. Many were amusing and ridiculous as well as pathetic and sad. Years after, Mrs. Anna Prime, an old colored woman, very dark, told me that she lived in New York at the time. She worked at service for a wealthy family on Madison Avenue in a brown stone house about middle of the block. The first day of the riot they noticed their house marked and removed the chalk or paint, went in and closed and darkened all windows, locked and barred all doors, and remained quiet in the back part and upstairs for nearly a week. Provisions and food gave out. The street appearing quiet, she said, "I volunteered to go to the grocery. The others protested but I, being young and brave, insisted. So, wrapped in a shawl with an old sunbonnet hiding my face, they let me out the basement door. Few people were in sight. I started to run. Turning the corner, I ran right into a crowd. Someone pulled off my bonnet (looked so odd) and hollered, 'See the Nigger.' I jumped and run back, no racehorse ever made such time. I jumped down the basement steps and bursted open the door, which was quickly closed and barred. But I was crazy, did not know anything for a week. Was I skeered? Well, I don't know what else to call it, for over a year I could pass for an albino (white face and hair) and even now after forty years the very thought of that night acts as a cathartic."

    Our life on the island was a forced banishment under many vicissitudes. It proved to be an educational and practical experience. The older of us learned much. We saw the criminal at close range in the penitentiary and workhouse brought there for crimes committed. We saw the alms house filled with hundreds of paupers, mostly old and decrepit, brought there after a wasted life and indiscretion. Many of them were educated and refined. They loved to talk to us boys and girls, telling their experiences, exploits on land and sea, of wealth and influence, but now only waiting for the end, to be buried in Potter's Field. Afterwards, their bodies would be dissected and experimented upon for the benefit of young doctors from Bellevue Hospital. We saw the insane, two thousand or more, exhibiting every phase of mental derangement, from raving mad men to the docile, speechless and demented, whose reason had been wrecked by as many causes as there are numbers. Oh, what a sight! What a lesson we learned from their afflictions.

In due time we received clothing and began to prepare to leave the island. The asylum managers had great difficulty in securing a property that was adapted to a home for the orphans, temporarily, until they could find a proper place. Finally, they secured the Fields Mansion at 152nd St. and 10th Ave. on the high land overlooking the Hudson River. It had been a most wonderful and beautiful place. To tell the facts and legends connected with the place would require a professional historian. It is necessary, however, that I should attempt at least an outline so that you may know where we went from the island, after a two month sojourn, being well fed, washed, clothed and entertained and enlightened, if you please.

I must make special mention of two or three friendships on the island. Mr. Anderson, the warden or general commissioner of charities, lived on the island. He had a splendid residence, modern in every detail, surrounded by beautiful flower gardens, etc. He had a fine boathouse furnished with several row boats, six oared barges, eight or ten men dressed as sailors on hand all the time to ferry the warden's family and friends back and forth over the river to 65th St. in the city.

Mr. and Mrs. Anderson were specially kind and gracious to us orphans. We were often taken to their home to sing and entertain their guests, and we fared well. They gave us clothing and nice eatables but no money for we could not use it. Mr. Anderson had made for me a fine cadet suit, dark blue cloth, the seams covered with red cord, with shoulder straps and cap.

We also had a dear friend in the person of Rev. Joseph Rosey, born blind, but had received a thorough theological education. He was a fluent speaker. He had a fine library with a Bible and many books with raised letters. He wrote his own sermons by a process of perforations through paper that he read with perfect ease. Although blind, his other four senses - hearing, feeling, tasting and smelling - were most acute, marvelous. He was stationed on the island to administer religious services to the paupers and criminals, under the auspices of a "Bible Society" in New York City. He was always neatly dressed in ministerial garb. He was a perfect Frenchman in appearance, polite and courteous. It was my pleasure to accompany him several times to the city as guide. He knew the city better than most New Yorker's with both eyes. He knew the buildings that he wished to visit and was very familiar with the hotels and restaurants. It did seem as though he had a perfect map of the city constantly before his eyes. He was especially interested in us children, giving us many talks and lectures that were most interesting and instructive. We left him with many regrets.

Mr. Simpson, the general overseer of the alms house, was indeed our friend, making our stay on the island a holiday in every sense. He was always planning for our pleasure and amusement. I will relate a couple of his acts that will illustrate him. He called it Marathon Race. He selected forty of the older boys and took us to the bake house where there were about two hundred empty flour barrels to be delivered to the steam boat landing about a quarter of a mile distant. There were splendid hard, oval white-shell roads, fifteen feet wide, with many curves. His scheme was that the boys must roll the barrels, not carry them, using hands and feet to push them along. Each boy would receive ten cents. The one delivering the greatest number of barrels to the dock would receive fifty cents, the next thirty, and the third twenty cents. He put forty numbers in a hat and blindfolded a boy who then distributed the numbers.

That gave the positions for the start; five in line and eight lines, five feet apart, each with a barrel in front of him. When all were ready, a pistol shot was the signal to start. We could go as fast as we wished but had to keep in the road, going or coming for barrels, or we were disqualified. The boys were in great glee and excitement. Simpson was a great organizer and disciplinarian. He had invited Miss Andrews and friends to witness the event; and they came, a dozen or more ladies and gentlemen.

All being ready, Mr. Simpson fired the pistol. All were off. Now, my reader, you must draw on your imagination. The scene begs description. Imagine forty colored boys, average age twelve years, clad only in pants and shirt. Some had two suspenders. It was on a hot afternoon in August, rolling empty barrels over an oval road, smooth, hard and white, contending for fifty, thirty and twenty cents. Each boy pledged to remain in the race until every barrel was delivered at the landing. No one has brains sufficient to imagine such a scene. The sound of the pistol had not died when there was a complete mix-up of barrels and boys, each striving to get ahead. Not a barrel went ten feet in the direction intended. Over they went, boy over barrel, barrel over boy, and such howling and screaming, a side-splitting scene. Soon all along the road there were different stages of disaster - crying from bruises, quarreling, sweating and youthful cussing. Finally the barrels were all delivered, perhaps two hours later. The writer was not one of the victors but very much scratched, bruised and exhausted. The visitors saw the sight of their lives and had brought us lemonade and small cakes. Simpson declared it a great success. We went down to the river, washed up and were happy.

The other act that I will always remember was a tragedy. We had two large two-wheeled carts, mounted with strong crate-like boxes about four feet high by six feet long with low, heavy wheels. They had double handles from back and front so that they could be run the same either way. We usually had six boys to a cart, three in front and three in back. On this day in question we had been over to the women's side delivering several hundred loaves of bread, perhaps a fourth of a mile. Mr. Simpson was with us. When the bread was delivered, we came out on the main road. He wanted to see some fun. The carts stood side by side, six boys for each one. He offered ten cents apiece to the crew that got to the bake house first. He started us over a splendid road with a little downgrade. We had to pass through a high stone wall. The gates were immense. The gatekeeper heard and saw us coming and opened wide the gates. We were running just as fast as possible, one cart just about a length ahead. Just as we were passing through the gates, an old woman, a pauper, stepped in front of the gateway to pass through. Not seeing or hearing us and as she was directly in our path, we could not stop or turn out but struck the poor woman square in the side. She had attempted to turn. Over she went, us on top, with both wagons. It was a terrible mix-up. The woman was knocked speechless. None of us were seriously hurt except for a few bruises. With much fright, we assisted the gatekeeper to carry the woman to the hospital nearby. We never heard her fate. It was an unavoidable accident. The gatekeeper and Mr. Simpson exonerated us, as she was on the wrong side of the wall. No one could see her, and we were making such noise. She must have been deaf and standing on the men's side of the big gates. This accident cast a gloom over us and stopped our wagon races.

Scarcely two weeks had passed when two of our boys went in bathing while the tide was going out. They, not being expert swimmers, were carried out to sea, and we never saw or heard from them. They both jumped in together and were never seen again. Thus we had two serious tragedies on the island.

One day in the later part of September 1863, we boarded the pretty little steamer "Belview." We retraced our voyage to Manhattan Island to the dock at the foot of 152nd St. on the Hudson River. What a contrast to our first trip on that black, somber police boat, armed with cannon, guarded by guns and soldiers with a cargo of hundreds of colored women and children, frightened and half naked, stowed away in the hull and not daring to speak above a whisper. By this date, the other refugees had gone their way to the city, leaving us, the children of the orphan asylum. When the day came for us to leave, which was a splendid autumn day, we were happy, had full stomachs, and were clothed in garments of many and varied fashion and color, but clean. The older children carried packages containing personal property or souvenirs. I had the hat and shirt that I wore through the riot, and I have the shirt today. After sixty-four years, the little old muslin shirt, once white, is yellow with age.

Arriving at the pier, we ran down the gangplank. No one needed help. Mr. Davis, Mr. Griffin and several other old attendants were with us as we went up the road, all expectant to see the new home. There it stood, on the brow of the hill, a majestic architectural edifice of stone and brick. Its architecture was a blending of the old and new to make it modern in front. It was a three-story building including the mansard. The back was five stories. It stood against the hill. In fact, both sides were front, facing the Boulevard (Broadway), the other facing the river. The grounds were spacious, about thirty acres, half level, the rest sloped to the river. The boundaries were as follows: on the north was 152nd St.; on the east was Broadway, the old Military Road, 100 feet wide, running from the Battery to Albany - after leaving the city proper it was called the Bloomingdale Road; on the south was 150th St.; and on the west was the Hudson River. It was a wonderful location, romantic and picturesque. The river, which was two miles wide with the tide and the palisades, perpendicular rocks 100 feet high, running as far as the eye could reach north and south on the Jersey shore, were the grandest scenic effects in the world.

Before trying to describe the building, I will relate what I know of its tradition. About one hundred years ago, or forty years before we went there, a man by the name of Fields bought the ground. He was rich from importation business from England and France, besides inherited riches. He was in the diplomatic service of the United States to France. He married a titled French lady, brought her to America, and built this beautiful mansion. After a few years of residence here, her health failed. They returned to Paris where she died.

The house was securely closed for twenty years, except for a few rooms in the basement occupied by a caretaker. I have not the ability to adequately describe its structure or furnishings. Everything was brought from France, with lavish expenditure. There were two entrances to the grounds, one from the Boulevard, through massive gates, with small sentinel or guardhouses on either side and a winding road through a beautiful grove. The other entrance was from 152nd Street. The approaches to the house were all through beautiful flower gardens, up wide, circling, marble steps. There were marble pillars on either side and great black walnut doors.

Upon entering, the vestibule led into a spacious court, tiled with black and white marble. On either side, wide semi-circular stairs led to the apartments above. Opposite the front door was a wide hall leading to the rear of the house; also from the court were four doors that opened into large rooms. Between each door were beautiful marble vases three or four feet high for natural plants or flowers. The ceiling of the court was a dome from which suspended a mammoth brass chandelier that would hold fifty or more candles. From this court also there were two or more glass doors opening out onto spacious verandas or porches. On the side walls, between each opening, were bracket candlesticks of brass. All the rooms on this floor were finished in a similar manner, white walls with beautiful plaster ornaments. There was no paint. The woodwork was all polished black walnut. Hinges, locks, and all metal trimmings were of polished brass or bronze.

The rooms on the next floor were much smaller, in suites of two or three, with wardrobe rooms or other closets. In practically all the larger rooms there were stationary divans or couches, beautifully upholstered in velvet or leather. Also in these rooms were great fireplaces with marble mantles of different colors, mounted with large plate mirrors, all stationary. In every room there were ideal, or family portraits or pictures with brass frames.

The third floor consisted of many small rooms, presumably servant quarters, all connected by a back stairway. In the attic apartment there were storerooms furnished with shelves, hooks, etc. There was a large copper water tank, 100-barrel capacity, which would hold the water from the roof or fresh water from a hydraulic ram down on the side hill, in a spring of excellent water.

The basement was one labyrinth of rooms for storage of food, wood, ice, utensils, laundry and kitchenware. There were no out buildings except the barn, and that had been constructed on the same elaborate plan for horses, cows, and poultry. There were spacious carriage rooms and coachman's quarters. This building, being of wood, had been almost destroyed. It still stood, but floors, roof, and under parts were rotten, falling in, and moss covered.

The twenty or more years that the grand residence had not been opened above the basement made it a dangerous place for the health of children. Our managers had, for weeks before we came, tried to air out and renovate; but it was poison, foul, with gasses from decay, a veritable pest house.

The once beautiful grounds laid out with artificial lakes, fish ponds, rustic bridges, the park with paths leading to grottoes and the river, were now rotten and covered with weeds, underbrush, and decay. The pools, not having outlet, were rank with decayed vegetation and filled with disease germs; everywhere in the woods was the original wilderness, infested with snakes, frogs, and the like, and stagnant pools and swamps. What a place for three hundred or more youngsters! We went wild from the close confinement of the home on 44th Street and at Blackwell's Island, where rigid rules prevailed. The wilds of 152nd Street were too much for us. Our managers, busy each day trying to get this place, this home, in convenient shape and building a schoolhouse, left us without restraint.

With all those acres of wilderness to traverse, the effect was soon felt. As the season advanced toward winter, rain and storms soon converted our new home into a hospital. What a time we had that winter, with every variety of sickness the human family could contract. Inflammation of the eyes was an epidemic along with whooping cough, seventy-six coughing at one time, bowel trouble, poison ivy, typhoid fever, throat trouble and everything else. Why not? We drank the water from those stagnant pools, ate the bad as well as good fruit, and waded in the marshes and swamps. I, always very healthy, was first taken with sore eyes, then whooping cough, and finally typhoid fever developed. I was put in a room with seven others, five of whom died. There were twelve deaths that winter. Dr. McCune Smith, with an assistant, was our physician. His health failed him. Dr. Frothingham succeeded him, a fine old man. It was kill or cure with him, rough and gruff. One night he took my temperature and pulse, rising from the bed and wiping his instruments, and he spoke to the nurse, Mrs. Titus, "Well, Thomas can't live; at the turn of the night, twelve o'clock, he will die." I was perfectly conscious, could hear and see, but could not speak or move and had no pain. The doctor said I would die, and I suppose he knew, but I had not the slightest idea of such a thing. I wanted to tell Mrs. Titus that I was thirsty and wanted something to eat but could not speak. I watched the clock, looking for the time to come. As twelve drew near, I saw Mrs. Titus's anxious looks and actions. She brought Mrs. Carter, another nurse, and they bathed my head with cold water and put a large spoonful of orange juice in my mouth. It went down, but I could not swallow. It felt and tasted so good. Mrs. Titus loved me as her own son, and as she watched and felt my pulse, I saw the tears in her eyes, but I could not speak. I tried so hard to tell her that I was not dying. I wanted her to kiss me and give me plenty of orange juice, but she did neither, just watched me. I lay there fighting off death with what willpower I had. Twelve o'clock came and there they stood over me, all attention. If he could only speak, they would say. I tried my best to call. The morning came and so did the doctor. The boy next to me had died. The doctor sat on my bed, examined me, and then, looking over at the dead boy, said,

"Too good, too good, on earth to stay," and looking at me he said, "Too bad, too bad, from earth to take away. Tom is going to live." Mrs. Titus asked, "Doctor, do you really think Thomas will live, get well?" and he answered, "Yes, you can't kill him." I certainly owe my life to Mrs. Titus. She gave me efficient and constant care. After three months, I came out of the hospital perfectly well but weak and emaciated.

The winter had been very severe, cold and snowy, having a salutary effect to remove germs and disease. The spring brought health and sanitary conditions. The management had completed a long, roomy wooden building for school purposes. Conditions had been wonderfully improved. I returned to school. The institution had received three scholarships to Oberlin College, a donation the year before. Then came a contest for selection among the boys. I won first position, but the doctor advised not to send me until the next year, when I had grown stronger.

Miss Annie Shotwell, the principal director, having a special interest in me, concluded to take me to spend the summer at her country home in the village of West Farms. So, about the first of June 1864, with an extra suit of clothes and the envy of the boys, I entered the lady's carriage in company with her and was driven about ten miles to her farm in West Chester County. It was a beautiful summer morning and started early with a lunch basket, driving slowly over dusty roads. We made several stops as she wished to call on friends en route.

We arrived late in the afternoon at "Murray Manor," an antiquated, colonial farm residence, two stories high, with huge pillars and dormer windows on the slanting roof. We were met on the steps and pleasantly welcomed by a young colored woman whose name was Nancey, the housekeeper. Upon entering, we came into a spacious hall, dividing the house, with a wide stairway leading to the floor above. One side was occupied by one family, the Murray's, and by Miss Shotwell on the other side.

I should introduce the reader to Miss Anna Shotwell by a description of her. She was a Quakeress, maiden lady, advanced in years, short in stature, not weighing over 100 pounds. She was of the positive Quaker type, of rare and exceptional mental ability, wealthy, and noted for philanthropy. She was one of the original founders and promoters of the Colored Orphan Asylum Association. She was to New York what Lucretia Mott was to Philadelphia. The two women were intimate friends and coworkers in all movements, national and local, for the betterment of humanity. From my first entrance to the institution I attracted her attention, and being made monitor (errand boy), was often sent to her city residence and thus won her good graces. I had studied hard to win the scholarship at the expense of my health. She took me away to recuperate. I lost my scholarship by going but gained robust health in the three months of country life. The Murrays and Shotwells were closely related, of old colonial families. The Murrays remained in the city and were seldom at the country house. So Miss Anna Shotwell, Nancey Smith, and Tommy Barnes were the occupants of the great big old farmhouse.

That evening, Nancey quickly prepared supper for us. It consisted of cold boiled ham, bread, butter, cheese, currant preserves, and hot tea. There were two small tables set. One was in the center of the large dining room for Miss Annie, with fine white linen cloth and damask napkin. The china was delicate and rare. The silver was heavy and of antique design, the whole being simple, neat and rich. Miss Annie came in and took her seat at the table with simple grace, dressed immaculately in her Quaker costume. You would not have dreamed that she had ridden ten miles over a dusty road. She looked much like a doll on exhibition, pausing for a moment in silent prayer. Nancey poured the tea then, at attention, stood near the chair. Miss Annie ate slowly but with appetite. Finishing her meal, she directed Nancey to remove the eatables to Tommy's table, which was nicely set but not so richly. I was supposed to be out in the barn or garden but had been quietly peeking in the window, closely observing every detail. When called, I came in, oh, how innocent! Miss Annie greeted me so nice, placing her hand on my shoulder, and said, "Thomas, you cannot be very hungry after that basket of food you ate on the road coming." She directed me to the table in the corner. Miss Shotwell had not the slightest idea of a thirteen-year old boy's appetite or capacity. I did not spend much time in silent prayer or formality. When I had finished, Nancey had nothing to put in the refrigerator. Miss Annie did not make me wait or put me at a separate table on account of color prejudice. She may have considered me her equal before God. I was not her equal intellectually or socially. I was not her servant but her ward, brought to her home for my special benefit, the improvement of my health and mentality. She had a servant in the person of Nancey Smith, a colored woman, who did not dine with us. The Quaker idea is not idleness, therefore, I was given tasks, not laborious work, and was expected to perform them promptly and efficiently; early to bed and early to rise being lived up to. She gave me books that were beyond my intelligence, but she took pains to explain them to me.

There was the daily routine of chores, study and religious worship (Bible reading and prayer), morning and night. Anna Shotwell was an ideal Christian, strictly adhering to the tenets of her creed, no "can't," no affectation, no emotional excitement. When dark came, Nancey showed me my room and my bed, up two flights of stairs to the attic or top floor. It had been previously arranged, a great spacious garret over the whole house about eight feet high in the center, sloping to about four feet on the side, with six large, dormer windows, two on each side and one on each end, looking out on the roof. The floor was bare except where the bed stood, and there was a strip of carpet on each side. The bedstead was old and old-fashioned with great round posts, head and foot board, corded to hold the straw-filled tick (mattress). It had two sheets, a light quilt and feather pillow, all scrupulously neat and clean. There was a small old table, cloth covered, with candlestick, candle and matchbox on it, and a quaint chair. Around the room there were several cabinets or clothes presses. On the walls were innumerable hooks or pegs hanging full of clothes, for men and women - great coats, heavy cloth dresses, gray, brown and drab. There were several massive oaken chests with great iron locks and hinges; old, old trunks, old chairs, tables, and other antique furniture and fixtures were all hung and arranged in painful order, no dirt, no dust, and no rubbish. Everything good but oh, so grim and quiet. My bed looked like a great white field. As it was growing darker, I lit the candle but oh my, it cast great shadows that frightened me. I blew out the light, then the twilight through those draped windows cast great figures across the floor; such deathly stillness. There I was, alone in that great garret room, afraid to lie down, afraid to stay up. I looked toward the stairway, thinking of flight, but it looked deep and dark. I dropped down on my knees beside the chair and prayed as I had never before or since. Stealthily I looked to the windows and then all around the room. Rising to my feet, a cold sense of security came over me. I stood, looking in every direction, a fearful silence. A few lines from Poe's famous poem "'The Raven" fully depict my position and emotions.

> "Deep in the darkness peering long I stood there, Wondering, fearing, doubting, dreaming dreams. No modal ever dared to dream before; but the Stillness was unbroken- the darkness gave no token The only word there spoken was the whispered word."

With me there was no word spoken, no echo. I may have whispered, "Mother." So, turning around, I got into bed in one corner, for it was large enough for a dozen my size. Then with my senses all alert, I lay there thinking of the past long winter, of the sickness, of how so many of my fellows had died, five of the seven in my room. Now I was well and growing strong. I had no feeling of sleep. I deliberately closed my eyes, thanked God for my life, my brother, my relatives and my friends who had been so good to me. Then the thought came to me, "Why should I worry?" Fear left me, and I lay there and peacefully fell asleep and dreamed of my mother, that she sat at my bedside. The details of that dream are as vivid now as that night sixty years ago and, reader, have it as you may, I firmly believe that it was my mother's influence that took the fear from me

Photos from the Colored Orphan Asylum

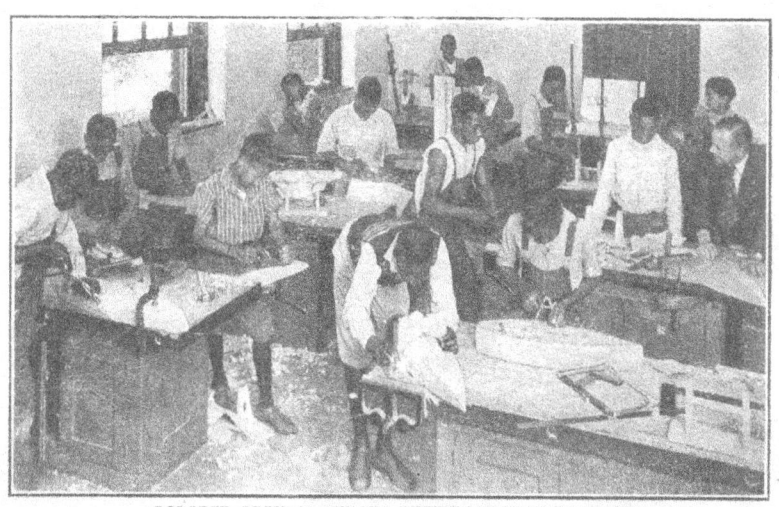

COLORED ORPHAN ASYLUM, RIVERDALE-ON-HUDSON, N. Y.

T. H. and Mary Belle Peoples Barnes

50th wedding anniversary, Olean, NY

Maria Lott, aunt of Mary Belle Peoples Barnes

T. H. and 1st-born, died in infancy

Rose Lott, grandmother of
Mary Belle Peoples Barnes

John Lott, grandfather of
Mary Belle Peoples Barnes

Peter Barnes, brother of
T. H. Barnes

Sarah Virginia Williams,
Mrs. Ireland,
Cousin of T. H. Barnes

Caroline Williams, wife of Peter A. Williams

Peter A. Williams, uncle of T.H. Barnes

Young T. H. and friend

Freddie Townsend and T. H.

T. H. and friends

T. H., Mary Belle and children at their 25th wedding anniversary

T. H. Barnes and grandson John Crawford, 1925
in T. H.'s barbershop, Olean, N.Y.

Memorial service at the Frederick Douglass monument, 1937

in that great attic room. I never was afraid after that.

Then morning came; I awoke at five, the usual time. I made my bed with the same precision that I found it, went around the room and made a hasty minute inspection. I saw nothing but good clothing, good furniture, and a demonstration of cleanliness and neatness so seldom seen in a garret. I went downstairs and told Nancey my night's experience. She had a good laugh. When Miss Annie appeared, I told her in detail. She was visibly affected and at prayers, she prayed that God would assist her to make me happy and contented.

Breakfast was about the same as supper, after which she took me all over the place, showing me a small garden of vegetables and flowers. Then she took me to Mr. Gibson, the man that ran the farm for her and lived just a short distance up the road.

He had a wife and two sons of eighteen or twenty years. He had a fine little farmhouse, good barn and all that appertain - horses, cows and chickens. The farm supplied the Murrays and Shotwells with vegetables, fruit, etc.

I was well pleased with the place, but it was so quiet and lonesome after years of daily association with hundreds of children and adults. The place with all its pleasant surroundings seemed a desert. I determined to be resigned to my situation. Miss Annie was all kindness and so anxious that I should be content. The days passed slowly but pleasantly. I had a schedule of routine chores - work in the garden, drawing water from the well, going on errands to the village, study and reading.

Sunday came (Sabbath, quiet day), nothing to do but read. In the afternoon three large coaches came (family carriages) filled with Quaker men, women and several young people, but they were as quiet as their elders. The occasion was Sabbath School in the parlor with Bible reading, questions asked and answered, and prayers but little singing. I was the observed of all observers. Miss Annie seemed proud to present me as one of her "Asylum Boys," brought there for improvement, physical and mental. They seemed very pleased to hear me read from the Bible and sing. They had a light lunch and started for home since they all seemed to live at a distance. I felt bad to see them go for the house would be more quiet and lonely than ever. Our house stood on a side road, not the regular thoroughfare, so there were few passersby. Nancey had gone to New York early in the day so I was alone. Miss Annie sat in the parlor, reading. I went early to bed after a long, long lonesome day.

The following week passed similarly except for one incident that broke the monotony which was interesting and amusing to me. I wore a cap of dark blue cloth, eight cornered, with a patent leather peak. It was very heavy for summer but was my best. While drawing water from the well one day, my cap fell in, so deep that I could not see it. Miss Annie was very much troubled and insisted on me getting it out as soon as possible as the water would spoil it because it contained much paste board to keep it in shape. I got a long pole and tried so hard to get it out but to no avail. I had to leave it overnight. Next day I called Mr. Gibson, the farmer. He brought a long pole with a hook. We worked until late in the afternoon but finally succeeded, much to Miss Annie's satisfaction. She insisted that much of the water be drawn out of the well for she did not relish using the water after that old cap had been soaked in it. Many buckets of water had to be drawn. Then she wanted Mr. Gibson and I to test for any cap flavor. We declared the water perfect, but Annie did not drink any for several days. Gibson, Nancey and I had a good laugh, and Nancey displayed her ingenuity by rebuilding the cap with new lining, paste board, etc. She teased Miss Annie by calling the water "cap soup."

Miss Annie told me that the next Sunday there would be a meeting (Quaker) at Fordham, about five miles distant. She expected the Murrays to drive up from the city, and she would ride with them; but not being sure, she would prepare to go otherwise.

I had previously told her that I could drive and well knew the care of a horse. She took me out to the barn and showed me a splendid old-fashioned carriage or coach. It was covered with oilcloth. The vehicle had not been used for several years and was very dusty. I told her that I could clean it perfectly as it was in good shape. She had faith in me and said she could get a horse in the village. So after she had gone in the house, I opened wide the inner barn doors and with heroic effort got the old ark out on the barn floor. I was delighted for I wanted something of the kind to do. I wanted to drive to Fordham. I wanted to show her what I could do. I had learned the art of horse and carriage care in the institution. So Friday morning, with Nancey's help, I secured clean cloths, soap, brushes and oil and went to work on the old coach. With new inspiration came pep. There was every convenience in the barn including wrenches and levers for removing the wheels. Nancey would come and help, giving a lift when needed. So late in the afternoon I had the old hack looking like new. I had rubbed and oiled the varnished parts, dusted well the cushions and upholstery, and polished the door handles, lamps and all the metal parts. Now I tell you, it was a rare old wagon fit for a queen. A coupe built for two to ride inside, two on the driver's seat. Nancey brought out Miss Annie. She was astonished; and had she not been a Quakeress void of demonstrative affection, she would have kissed me. She actually smiled, looking the picture of suppressed pleasure and delight. She exclaimed, "Why Thomas, thou hath done remarkably, thou art a genius, made the carriage new." I covered the coach, closed the barn door, washed up, had a good supper, for my appetite was keen, and went to bed to sleep until daybreak, Saturday morning.

The real work had done me good. I felt splendid and went down to the village to see the man to furnish the horses. He was just hitching up to go to work. He was surprised to see me so small. I was surprised to see the horse so large. It was white, quite young, in good condition, but great Scott, how dirty and stained! He was hitched before a two-wheeled dirt cart. I saw he had good spirit, which pleased me. The man questioned me much about my ability to drive. I soon convinced him that I was expert. He told me he would be home early, and I could get the horse about three o'clock. Going back home, I told Miss Annie. She was pleased and showed that she had perfect confidence.

After the morning routine - devotion, breakfast and chores - three o'clock soon came. I was at the horse barn. He soon drove in and wanted me to drive the horse and cart up to my barn, but I did not want the cart, so unhitched. But to my surprise and chagrin he told me that was the only harness he had. It was a great heavy cart harness. When I reached home, Mr. Gibson was there. He laughed loud and long at the harness for the fine carriage. I went with him to the barn, picked up some odds and ends of harnesses and with what I found in our barn, rigged up a very creditable harness. I went to work in earnest with soap, water, and blacking on the outfit. I knew Miss Annie would not tolerate any work Sunday morning so got Nancey to help me. We got down to business on horse and harness, gave the animal a good feed with a couple of apples, patted him, and soon we were the best of friends. And such a scrubbing that horse never got before. We made him clean. Although his hair was like scarlet, we made it white as snow. Nancey was big and strong; she caught my enthusiasm and did as I directed. She neglected her own Saturday work to assist me. I owe my success to her. Gibson helped me with the harness adjustments, straps and polishing of buckles. Long before dark Gibson, Nancey and I had accomplished a transformation, from a dirty cart horse to a perfectly groomed carriage horse. I had trimmed his fetter locks and mane, blacked his hooves, wrapped him in a clean blanket and gave him a good bed of straw. That horse must have had dreams of being a royal charger.

Sunday morning I was up with the larks. I got out my Sunday suit, blacked my shoes, made everything ready, then went to feed my horse. On looking over the outfit, a new horror seized me. Those shafts looked too small. I brought out the horse and so, lo and behold, they were entirely too small for that big horse. The carriage had been built for two horses. The shafts put on had belonged to a phaeton. What to do? I did not know and did not want to tell Miss Anna my plight. So I just ran over the field to Gibson. He saw me coming and thought something serious had happened by my excitement. I told him my trouble, and he sat down and laughed and said, "I thought of that myself yesterday but forgot to speak of it. We will go to the next farm house; perhaps they can help us out." Up to the next farm we went, half a mile or more. The farmer took us out to his wagon house, and there was a large pair of shafts, good but dirty. We took them to the well, gave them a good washing, and they looked fine. We promised to return them on Monday and started back with our prize. They did not exactly fit the carriage, but we made a good connection on one side of the axle and wired the other side. We wrapped the coupling neatly with black cloth on both sides. Gibson helped me hitch up for I was fatigued from excitement. When complete, everything looked A No. 1, and I was an hour ahead of time to start.

Making myself ready, I called Nancey for inspection. She pronounced everything perfect, so I drove out to the front door. Miss Annie was waiting. With true footman etiquette, I helped my lady into her coach, holding the reins in my left hand. The horse was chaffing at his bit. The lady noticed this and said, "Thomas, canst thou drive that horse with safety?" I assured her. Then getting on the box, sitting square in the center of the seat, my feet dangling, for my legs were not long enough to reach the floor, we were ready to start. Miss Anna Shotwell, the personification of dignity, sat upright on the seat. I detected an expression of doubt. The horse, feeling good, started off on an easy trot. The coach was a plaything for him. Miss Anna called me, "Thomas, thou must not drive fast. This is the Lord's Day, and the sun is very warm for the horse." The fact is I was perfectly confident of driving safely, but I could not prevent the horse's trotting. He felt good, had a light load and a fine road. We had not gone over a mile when we came up to a great, cumbersome coach with two horses, jogging along very moderately. My horse turned out to go by. I could not stop him. He obeyed every move of the lines in turning out, but I could not check his gait, and past we went. The occupants of the coach were a Quaker family of five. They bowed to Miss Shotwell and she to them. I knew she would think me rude for passing them as we did. When she saw what was happening, she spoke in a low but animated voice, "Thomas." I knew what it meant. Some distance ahead, I saw another similar outfit. The horse, continuing his easy trot, brought us nearer and nearer. I heard that voice, "Thomas." I know what that meant, this time louder than before. Then I concluded that something must be done. So, sliding down from my seat, my feet on the floor, I immediately saw my advantage and, drawing up sharp on the lines, my horse slacked up and not any too soon for we were right up to the rig ahead. The horse wanted to pass but now I was master of the situation and held him back. He acted splendidly. By this time there were several carriages and vehicles ahead. We were drawing near the village. I could see the meeting house and people assembling. I would have drawn up in front of the door and let my lady out, but she told me to drive under the shed, this side of the church, where other coaches were standing, so I did. A man, standing near, came over to us, opened the door and, in a very friendly tone, said, "Anna, how do you do?" She answered by calling his name. I got out, took my horse fast to the manger, and came back to meet her. She took me to one side, and I expected a reprimand but instead she spoke very pleasantly, "Thomas, I understand, but you should never drive by an elder without permission."

There were twenty-five or more carriages, well fitted and filled with Quakers young and old. Each knew the other. All were friends, shaking hands and calling each by his or her first name. There was no "Mr." or "Mrs."; greetings and short pleasant talks followed.

All went into the meeting house, a rather low, one-story building, painted white with windows on all sides, much resembling a country schoolhouse, plain, without any embellishment or ornament. The interior, one large room, had bare floors, chairs, and benches all around against the wall and a few in the center. There was a small table at one end with a pitcher, pail of water, glasses, a Bible and small books, perhaps hymnals. When all were seated, women on one side, men on the other, there was profound silence for five or ten minutes. Then a woman went to the table and began speaking in a very moderate tone of voice for a short time. Then another and another, men and women, until many had spoken. A passage of scripture was read and talked about. There did not seem to be any particular leader. When quiet came, quite a number got up and walked around in single file. Then they were seated for a silence, then all mingled in friendly conversation. The whole affair seemed informal or as the spirit moved them. After good-byes were said, they returned to their carriages and departed their several routes. This, to the best of my memory, is correct.

Miss Shotwell seemed proud or pleased to present me as a boy from the Orphan Home. All seemed to know. They greeted me very cordially.

On the road home, I had hard work keeping the horse down to a slow trot. He was anxious to go fast, really delighted with conditions. About noon, the sun hot, the road dusty, both horse and driver sweating, with Miss Shotwell sitting erect and dignified, we arrived home safe and sound. Nancey came to meet us at the gate, all expectant to know of the trip. Miss Anna was as loud in her praise as her dignity would permit.

I put the horse in the barn and made him comfortable and returned him to the owner Monday morning. The man was delighted beyond expression at the horse's fine appearance and with the dollar for service, and he wished us to come often. Mr. Gibson came over in the evening to see if all had gone well.

Monday morning came with a new vision or duty, Nancey's wash day. It was every other week. The laundry was in the cellar, equipped with every convenience of the old type or style - rain water cistern, wood stove or charcoal. Nancey offered to do my washing - four shirts, stockings and handkerchiefs. I insisted on doing the trick myself, and astonished the women by getting all done by one o'clock, washed, dried and ironed. Miss Annie questioned me and I told her my mother had taught me to do housework and I had learned the laundry stunt in the institution. The care of a house was part of a boy's education. Right here I will advise every boy to acquire the domestic science, as often during life he will find it mighty handy and convenient.

As time passed my hair, being of that peculiar texture exceptional to colored people, grew long and unmanageable. I spoke to Miss Anna about it. She gave me twenty-five cents, the price then of a haircut. Mr. Gibson directed me to a barbershop in the village, located in a triangle building. Saturday morning, donning my best clothes, I started for the shop. Neither Miss Annie, Gibson nor I had any idea of race prejudice in that place, so into the Dutchman's barbershop I went. I took a seat to wait my turn. The barber, having his back towards me, did not notice who came in, so spoke aloud, "Take a seat, no one ahead." When he turned and saw me, his excitement knew no bounds. He stepped towards me, speaking in a loud voice, "Vot in h--l you vaunt in here?" Although much startled by his abruptness, I answered, "My hair cut, if you please." He had grown into a rage. He grabbed a long strap and, with an oath, rushed towards me like a mad bull. "You damned nigger, git out of here. Go to Abe Lincoln. He'll cut your hair." In a second, I was out in the street. He had followed me to the door with more oaths. I quickly returned home, telling Miss Anna word for word what had happened. She was horrified. She was nonplussed, had never heard anything like that before. She told me to go and tell Gibson out in the field. I repeated it to him. He lay down on a pile of hay and laughed loud and long. It was a huge joke to him. "Well, Thomas," he said, "I will have to fix you out." So that evening, over in the barn, he cut my hair off with sheep shears, then it was Nancey's laugh. She said I looked like the devil and tried to improve the cut with a dull pair of shears. She swore a light swear. Nancey was not pious and went through the daily prayer service about the same as washing dishes. It had to be done.

Fourth of July was nearing. I was very anxious to return to the Asylum, if only for a day. Miss Annie was not in favor of it. Knowing that I was very homesick, she feared I would not return, but finally she consented, with my promise to return the next day. It seemed the week would never pass. The morning of the third, Miss Annie (to my surprise) told me to get ready and go that day so as to spend the whole Fourth of July with my brother. She gave me seventy-five cents, twenty for railroad fare over and back and the balance for spending money. I was very happy and after dinner I was ready. Miss Annie gave me some official papers for Mr. Davis, the Superintendent. Gibson told me of a shortcut across to the river, so I concluded to walk and save the money. Taking my time, I arrived at the institution about six p.m. and received a wonderful welcome from everyone. The children flocked around me, asking a million questions. Miss Young and all of the teachers congratulated me and seemed pleased to see me so much improved. My brother was so glad that he cried, for we had never been parted before. I divided my money with him so that dried his tears.

The next morning we were up at daylight and had one big day. Mr. Griffin, Superintendent, had a good laugh over my haircut experience. He took me in the washroom and cut it over again. He was an expert at it. The next day came the trial. I had promised Miss Annie I would return to West Farms. She had been so good to me. I could not and would not disappoint her. So I bade all good-bye. With permission from Mr. Davis, my brother and several other boys walked a mile or more with me. I had quite a bundle to carry for I was taking back books and other things I needed. I could not walk fast so it was quite dark when I reached Miss Shotwell's. The old lady was delighted to see me. She had become attached to me and feared

I would not return. She sat down beside me, asking many questions to learn how I felt. I did like her, but my visit had spoiled me. I grew more and more homesick each day.

On the quiet, I wrote home to my Aunt Caroline in Brooklyn, asking her to come and see me. As soon as she received my letter, she came and saw my plight. She and Miss Annie had a long talk and agreed that it would be better for me to leave as they feared my health. In a few days I received a letter containing a dollar bill with instructions to come to Brooklyn and also a letter for Miss Annie. She gave me a good long talk, prayed for me, gave me a dollar and a nice, old-fashioned knife. Nancey was sorry to have me go, gave me twenty-five cents and the address of her people in New York, and made me promise to come and see her there. Kissing me, she bid me goodbye and turned away.

Miss Annie had ordered Gibson to drive me to the institution; she gave me a letter to Mr. Davis, the Superintendent. Before getting into the wagon, she held my hand long, advising, directing, and admonishing me. Thus I left Miss Anna Shotwell, a sainted woman. Why is it that there are not more like her? To those who have means, the opportunity is so great to make the less fortunate comfortable. I never met her again, but I cherish her memory and proclaim her praise. On the road over, Gibson was quite talkative. One sentence I will always remember. "Tommy, you ought to have remained with Miss Shotwell." He meant more than the words imply.

At the Asylum, Mr. Davis made out my discharge papers and with them gave me another long talk. He and I were much together. On 5th Avenue I always accompanied him downtown with the wagon for supplies, etc. I brought the milk every morning, 90 to 120 quarts from the Harlem and New Haven Depot at 48th and 49th Streets.

I remained at the institution a couple of days. I wanted to go home to my Aunt but oh, how I did regret leaving my brother and Miss Young, yes, everyone. What a parting! I will never forget. Many of the older girls and boys cried with me. I left my dear home after nearly five years of love and happiness. God will certainly bless forever the founders and supporters of that grand institution that gave hundreds, yes thousands, of children food, clothing, education, and happiness that would have otherwise lived and died in wretchedness.

Before leaving my old home in this narrative, I have much to say, more than time, space and ability will permit. If I am tedious or uninteresting, my readers must be charitable. Should I write volumes, I could not do my old friends justice. Time has removed them from this stage of action, but thank God there are others who have taken their place and continue the great, good work in a wonderful, successful manner. The present Colored Orphan Asylum at Riverdale on the Hudson is an Eden, a paradise.

I know of but one of the inmates that enjoyed the home with me, now living. He is John A. Doran, living at 52 West 8th Street, New York, 76 years old, six months my senior. I discovered him two years ago through Dr. Pitman, present Superintendent of the institution. We had not met nor did we know that the other lived for over sixty years.

The joy and emotion of our meeting cannot be described. We had been schoolmates, classmates, under our beloved teacher, Mary A. Young. John was a full orphan. As per rule, when he arrived at the proper age, he was bound or indentured to a farmer to remain until of age. Unfortunately, his employer was a cruel, heartless man who shamefully mistreated him and put him in a barn to sleep. The weather being rigidly cold, the boy's feet and hands froze, and he lost fingers and toes, making him a miserable cripple for life. The managers of the institution, learning of the boy's plight, brought him back and instituted legal proceedings. The money was deposited in favor of the boy, the institution as guardian. After being healed and restored to health, Doran was placed with another employer. Shortly after, the Asylum was burned by a mob.

He, hearing that it had been completely destroyed and abandoned, concluded that his interest was lost. When he was of age, he became a seafaring man for thirty or more years. He settled in Philadelphia. After years, his wife and children having died and he had grown old, he returned to New York and, in time, learned that the Asylum was still in existence. He made a trip to the Home and was identified. The managers immediately contributed to his needs and guaranteed permanent care. When we discovered each other, of course, an unexpressed friendship was cemented. We plighted a vow that while life should last we would forever keep in close communication.

The Colored Orphan Asylum is now in its eighty-seventh year and has cared for and educated more than six thousand children. What a wonderful record! Its projectors could not have dreamed of such a result. John Doran and Thomas Barnes are the oldest known recipients and beneficiaries of the great struggle of benevolence and philanthropy of that noble band of women originators. Are we thankful? God knows we are. Do we appreciate? Words cannot express our gratitude. Do we remember? Yes, as long as we live, those names we revere - Shotwell, Murray, Underwood, and Phelps.

Our prayers are thanksgivings, that there are just as devout and earnest men and women continuing the great work. The real story, the real impulse, that actuated the founders has been written and published, but in a very modest form, not giving the two young women, Shotwell and Murray, any credit. The narration of facts in detail are wonderful, interesting and inspiring.

I had the tradition from Miss Shotwell in person who, while I was at her home three months, took great pains to teach me the history, manners, and customs of the Society of Friends. One of their customs was that of a young friend, Quaker, accepting or adopting one certain or species of charity and fulfilling it for life. The two girls, by accident, met two small Negro children, orphans, destitute and homeless. Inquiring into conditions pertaining to such children, they found them revolting on account of race prejudice. They accepted the children as their wards, and thus were the first inception of the Home for Colored Orphans.

Later on I will write the full story as verified by Miss M. A. Young, a Quakeress and our teacher. It was her policy every Friday afternoon to teach and read politics, national events, history, tradition, little or no fiction. She delighted in rehearsing the origin of the Society of Friends (purely English), their trials, tribulations and successes, their martyrs, great men and women, Margret Fell, Lucretia Mott, Anna Shotwell and others. She repelled the word "Quakers" as derision or a nickname, given a certain faction of the Friends, who gave vent to their religious emotions by shaking or quaking. Miss Shotwell also insisted on the term "friends" (Society of Friends).

In the institution there were other race exponents. Mrs. Osborne, a teacher, born in Londenderry in the north of Ireland, was persistent in extolling the merits and accomplishments of her people, Protestant, Presbyterian Orangemen, educated and cultivated. She had nothing in common with the ignorant far down Corkonians. She added much to our knowledge of Irish history. Mrs. Osborne was one fine lady. I often quote her stories and sayings.

Mrs. Walker, our dining caterer, is often in my mind. She was Scotch and Scotch entire. She delighted in getting us lads and lasses in the room in the evenings, when we were supposed to be in bed, and sing Scotch ditties, quote Bobby Burns and, when occasion permitted, would dance the Highland Fling. She would tell us of Mary, Queen of Scots, give us good things to eat and send us off to bed on the quiet. Then "if a laddie kiss a lassie going through the hall, nara lassie squall."

Then there was Miss Clark, a diminutive Welsh lady teacher, always pleasant, kind and very devout, whether at play or school, always admonishing us to be good Christians. Aside from our school activities and routine, we had many side events to enlighten us. Especially do I remember an elderly gentleman that often came, taking a class of boys and with his little hammer trying to break all the rocks in upper New York teaching us geology. It was instructive and a recreation. One winter we had an expert in physiology, and he spoiled many an evening's sport by hanging his human skeletons and mannequins around our playrooms, frightening the life out of the younger set.

Some liberal friends donated twenty tickets to see the great horse tamer, Rarey, at the Academy of Music. It was fine. He would take the most vicious horse and make him perfectly gentle in ten minutes. Biters and kickers did it no more after his short treatment. Broncos and wild horses would follow him like pet dogs. A halter, small whip and mental control were his implements. Several times we went to Barnum's Museum for special attractions and also the old original Hippodrome to see genuine Roman Chariot races and horsemanship. On Saturday, we went to Central Park to hear the then famous Dodworth Band consisting of one hundred pieces. Often by the munificence of some benevolent friend we would have the pleasure and benefit of other educational transactions to Hoboken, Staten Island and Coney.

After war was declared, it was our privilege night after night to watch and see the march of thousands of troops to and from the barracks up Fifth Avenue and be lulled to sleep by the steady tramp and martial music. Oh, those days of thrills and excitement! We were awakened at midnight by the cry of the newsboy, "Extra, extra! Fort Sumpter has been fired on. Major Anderson holds the fort." Then there was the march of countless soldiers. Then came the horrible tragedy of July 13, 1863, burning our home. Can we forget? No, never, and they branded us as the innocent cause of the war.

The superintendent's residence, although an annex, was of the general city style, two-story, basement and high front steps, dormer windows from the roof, with improvements to date. Mrs. William E. Davis was a typical English lady, looked and lived the part. She was rather tall, had a dark complexion, black wavy hair combed down over the ears, with a cluster of cuds on either side, always attractively dressed in a style of a past decade, usually black silk, broad lace collar and cuffs, large cameo breast pin. I describe her minutely for she was a unique personage to me, always affable and pleasant but formal. Her husband's duty as superintendent of the Asylum was his personal business. She paid little or no attention to it. Her household was her domain. She often entertained, not lavishly but with dignified grace, her church associates. The education of her daughters and sons was paramount. The oldest son, married, was a principal in a city school. Miss Rosey, her eldest daughter, was a teacher in the Asylum. There was a younger daughter at a seminary and a boy at college. It was Mrs. Davis's habit for her social events to have Fannie Wright or myself as ushers. She had us well trained, dressed immaculately, standing at attention, the personification of the English lackey or footman, and we enjoyed it immensely. We were the recipients of tips and special attention from the guests, and I can say that the knowledge thus attained has served me well in later years.

I was present to do duty at the door. Early in the afternoon the doorbell rang. I answered it. There stood a woman, middle-aged, clean but very plainly clad. She asked for Mrs. Davis. I seated her in the vestibule; not having a card, I went down to the kitchen where Mrs. Davis was busy. I informed her that there was a lady waiting in the vestibule for her. "Thomas, show the lady into the parlor to be seated and tell her that I will be there in a few minutes; you remain in the hall," she said. I did as ordered. Mrs. Davis, with all haste, ran up the back stairs to her room to prepare her toilet. Presently, she came tipping down the front stairs with all the grace and dignity at her command and, with silk rattling, she stepped into the parlor. Seeing the poorly dressed old lady, she almost fainted with surprise. Regaining her composure, she addressed the woman civilly but coolly. When the stranger was dismissed, Mrs. Davis came to me all perturbed. "Why Thomas, you told me that there was a lady waiting for me. She was not a lady, only a very common woman. I must teach you the difference. Of course, here in America any woman of character and education is called a lady; not so in England. There, to be a lady, she must be of the royal family, a woman of title, a duchess or countess. A common woman of that cast in England would feel offended if you called her a lady. She would think you were making fun of her. Although I have lived in America many years, I am still an English woman and adhere to their customs." In conclusion, she admonished me to always treat all women with respect and courtesy, not question dress or character.

I must not forget to speak of Mrs. Penton. She was a nurse in the old hospital on 44th Street. Like Mrs. Howard, she boasted of her first family of New York, her lineage and her culture. It was a pardonable pride for there was, prior to the war, a very distinct class of colored people, sprinkled through the eastern cities from Baltimore to Boston, who were well educated, refined and aristocratic. If not always in possession of ample funds, they doted on a lineage mighty close to the Plymouth Rock. The war brought shoddyites, colored as well as white, making the dollar prevail instead of merit or blood. Mrs. Penton had a son named Robinson, born with deformed feet. They were successfully operated on in the institution, and he was made to walk quite natural. Robinson was a phenomenal scholar, often baffling and surprising his teachers. He grew up to be a lawyer and was admitted to the bar, but color prejudice kept him back.

There were other attachments in the Asylum that I should speak of but space will not permit; perhaps in the future the opportunity will come. They were all a Godly host and well merited our everlasting gratitude. On leaving, I carried many souvenirs, gifts and rewards won in school contests, etc. I still have three or more books brought from the institution - "School Days of Eminent Men," "The Vicar of Wakefield" and "William's Step-Mother."

Now I have related briefly my life and experience at the Colored Orphan Asylum. Leaving there opened a new epoch in my life.

My Uncle and Aunt most affectionately received me to an

exceptionally good home. Then came the rehearsal of the wonderful events of the past two years. They were eager for details of life in the institution, its routine, the mob tragedy, my sickness and sojourn at West Farms, all of which I gave minutely. My people often came to see us during the years at the institution but always on visitor's day. They got the impression that those days were specially prepared. That was a fact, but we children never enjoyed visitors except for the money we sometimes received; otherwise there was too much dress parade and strict discipline. We were happier without those days. These narratives were our evening entertainment. They also had a tale to tell, especially the riot horror.

The next day, Tuesday, they heard with consternation that the asylum had been burned and many killed and wounded. They could not go to us for they were in dire apprehension of meeting the same fate. Their house had been marked also. My grandfather, 78 years old and quite infirm, was placed in a store box, perforated, and carted as freight to pier #3 North River and put aboard a sound steamer, the Empire State. He was taken out more dead than alive from suffocation. There were a number of colored people employed on the steamer. As soon as practical, they moved out into the stream and anchored there for over a week, communicating with land at night with small boats. The family made the house dark and went to Weeksville, a suburb of Brooklyn, remaining there for two weeks. It was ten days before they learned of our miraculous escape. As soon as advisable, they obtained permission and visited us at Blackwell's Island.

After being at home a couple of weeks, a friend of the family, T. B. McKeal, proprietor of a restaurant on Fulton Street opposite the City Hall, induced my Uncle to let me go as cash boy for him at three dollars per week. I saw and learned much and soon grew into the good graces of the proprietor, waiters and all, perhaps fifty in number. I was pleased and got along splendidly, but I was anxious to learn a trade. On account of color prejudice, I was forced to accept that of a barber. On the fourth of October, Aunt and I left Jersey City en route to Susquehanna Depot over the Erie Railroad, a distance of two hundred miles. We had previously corresponded with Samuel T. Johnston, a distant relative, a barber, and he agreed to take me as an apprentice. He was much surprised and disappointed to see me so short in stature, weighing just seventy-five pounds. I was anxious to stay so after a couple days' visit it was agreed to let me stay two months, until Christmas. Aunt returned home. Johnston had a good country town barbershop with three chairs. He had a fine home, a wife and three small children, his being the only colored family in town. He was a man of good education, intelligent, a good public speaker and very popular. Mrs. Johnston was very motherly and kind to me. She would play and sing for me as I had several intermittent spells of homesickness, but I had the will to overcome them. Johnston was a musician and leader of an orchestra. The business took him out of town frequently. He soon made me "Charge d'Affairs" in his absence.

All went well until Christmas week. I told him that Aunt had sent me money to come home. He was apparently agitated and in replying said, "No, Thomas, your Uncle wants you to remain with me. I want you to stay, and I believe you want to stay yourself." I said, "Well, you told Aunt that I was altogether too small for a barber and would not answer, so I agreed to stay for awhile as I wanted to see the great railroad, shops, etc." He laughed. "I did say that. It was my first impression, but I have changed my mind. I need you." So we compromised by me going home for the holidays and returning.

On arriving home, all were pleasantly surprised to learn that Johnston wanted me to return. Aunt had secured another place for me at Fall River, Massachusetts, but fate decreed otherwise, for my benefit. After a two-week visit, Uncle returned with me to Susquehanna. He and Johnston mutually and legally bound me as an apprentice barber for three years and six months without pay. At the expiration of the term, I was to receive fifty dollars and a kit of tools as specified. I was to furnish my own clothes the first year and receive nine months of public school. All being amicably settled, Uncle went back home.

I determined to learn as fast as possible. When the school term began, he sent me to a private school called the Susquehanna Normal Institute. He said he wanted me to have the best and was willing to pay for it. The first day, I had a terrible time. The scholars, all older than myself, mutineered. Forty-five walked out, declaring that they would not go to the same school with a "nigger." The principal, Captain Rodgers, who had been an Army officer and resigned on account of his health, was resolute and determined. He told the striking pupils to go if they wished. They had paid the term fee; he was there to fulfill his part. "This boy has paid his, and he will stay if I have but one scholar." Seeing the determination of the principal, they held a consultation and concluded to stay and make it all so disagreeable for the nigger that he could not stay. Seven would not consent but took books and left. Three of this number came back in about a week. At noon, I told Johnston what had happened. He said, "Well, Thomas, Rodgers is with you. I have paid; it is up to you. All you need is 'sticktoitiveness'." So I made up my mind quick, knowing that it was my last chance at school, and at public school I would get no defense. So at one o'clock I was about two blocks away from the school building, hiding behind a fence. I saw that the boys and some girls were waiting to stone and beat me, so I concluded to wait until they had gone in. Rodgers saw their movements and remained at the gate until I came up. He grasped my hand saying, "I like your pluck. I was afraid you would not come back. I will fully protect you on the grounds but outside of that I have no jurisdiction. When school closes in the afternoon, you go when I give the signal. They will not know and you will have a start."

When he raised his hand, I had my books tied, hat in hand, and skipped downstairs. Many of them followed me. When I was out the gate, they gave me a volley of sticks and stones and such names as those intelligent young Americans could think. These fine young men and women were studying to be teachers. They had graduated from the public school and were now taking post- graduate courses in preparation for teaching. There was a small minority that protested against the treatment I was receiving. The second morning, in the large room, before going to classrooms a girl by the name of Mary Ryan asked permission to speak. In no moderate tone of voice she called the young men and women that stoned me miserable cowards and pointed her finger at them crying, "Shame, shame." Two or three tried to retaliate but most of them wilted. Several said that they were sorry, that they did not intend to hurt me but wanted to see me run. Mr. Rodgers spoke in the most seething and denouncing terms, "Thomas Barnes is the youngest and smallest scholar of the seventy-two on my roll. Your acts in the past two days have been a disgrace to me and my school. I hope there will never be a repetition," and there never was. Several would shun me, but soon I had many warm friends and I got along splendidly, taking three successive terms, nine months. I was invited to their social events and became a favorite of teachers and pupils.

That summer at one of their picnics, they were playing a game with twenty or more boys and girls in a circle. The scheme was to drop a handkerchief behind someone. That was a challenge to kiss the party if you could catch them. One of the girls dropped her handkerchief behind me, and I grabbed it. She ran like a deer, but I caught her and kissed her good; came back blushing. Some of the boys laughed and tried to jeer her. She stood still, looked at them and said, "I would rather have him kiss me than any of you fellows." I could relate many similar amusing incidents.

While in Susquehanna, I attended the Presbyterian Church and Sunday School. I had a good home. The Johnstons treated me like one of their own. Mr. Johnston took special pains to teach me and gave every advantage advisable. After three years, he consulted with me, stating that he intended to cut off the remaining six months and make me an equal partner in a barbershop at Great Bend,

Pennsylvania, nine miles distant. This I accepted very graciously, and I did a fine business for two years. I was indeed fortunate to be placed with such a man as Mr. Johnston. While he was not a professed Christian, he had the Christian spirit and demonstrated it to a wonderful degree. I would like to give in detail many interesting events during my apprenticeship. Finally I bought Johnston's interest in the Great Bend shop and ran it myself for several months, then sold out and went to Yonkers, New York with my Uncle who had started an elegant shop on Getty Square with four chairs. He wanted me to conduct it, and I was very successful.

The family had gone to Jackson, Mississippi as teachers in the Alcorn University. This was during the reconstruction period after the war bringing in the seceded states. After I had been a year or more in Yonkers, they wrote for me, having secured a nice position in the Mississippi legislature for me. I sold the shop. They advised me to wait until cool weather, September, before starting south. So I concluded to rest during the summer. I went to Elmira for a couple of months.

About September 1, 1870 I received a telegram that they all had been given ten days to leave the state by order of the Ku Klux Klan. "A word to the wise is sufficient." I changed my plans and went to Rouseville in the Pennsylvania oil fields. I ran a shop there for six months. Then I went to Tideoute, Pennsylvania to take charge of a shop for a friend while he went visiting. He did not return, so I gained possession of a good business practically for nothing. Fate or fortune favored me. It had been my intention to return to Yonkers, but having a location, a lucrative trade, and many friends I learned to like the place. One day a large, portly, elderly colored man came into my shop. His name was John Lott and his business was hauling crude oil. He owned several teams and was prosperous. He was loud in speech, abrupt in his manner, and his clothes were saturated with oil and mud. He hailed me. "Say, young fellow, I have heard of you, a tenderfoot from New York, and have come to look you over as colored young men of any kind are very scarce in these parts." I invited him to take a seat. We soon interested each other. I found him to be a man of more than ordinary intelligence. He had spent years in Haiti in import and export trade and had been lured to the oil country in search of gain and strange adventure. He stated that he was seventy but in robust health, which he displayed, and also told me of his family living in an adjacent oil town two miles distant called Babylon. At parting, he laid his hand on my shoulder saying, "Barnes, this is a very cold day, some below zero. Now, it is my habit in this kind of weather, at this time of day, and at my age to take a good drink for stomach's sake/ so he did. Then he gave me a very cordial invitation to call at his home, inadvertently mentioning his daughter and granddaughter of 16 and 17 years of age. The old gentleman called on me whenever in town, and there soon developed a real friendship. He loved to relate his adventures and exploits. He was an attentive listener to my simple stories, so we got along splendidly. Also, we were opposite in general appearance but two hearts that beat as one.

The weather being so extremely cold, when spring came the roads were so bad that it was nearly three months before I could visit the Lott home. It was up a long steep hill over two miles distant. I was eager to make the trip. So at last, a convenient Sunday came. My hotel was just opposite the post office. I had caught a glimpse of two sprightly damsels of banana complexion at the post office. They cast furtive glances in my direction. I divined their object. I made the pilgrimage to the Lott shrine, was greeted most cordially and ushered in most unceremoniously (concluded that I had been expected) to the sitting room to the presence of Miss Mary Belle Peoples (Lott). Since she was alone, we had to introduce ourselves. After the proper salutations and remarks in regard to weather, scenery, hills and valleys, oil derricks, etc., our conversation drifted in the line of personal research - how long have you been here, how long are you going to stay, do you like the oil region, do you get lonesome, etc.

I had an important errand to transact. A young man in Rouseville, a Mr. Catterdon, had separated from his wife in a quarrel while Miss Lott was present. The wife took off her wedding ring and threw it on the table. Neither would take the ring so they instructed Miss Lott to take the ring and keep it until called for. Months passed. The young man, learning that I was going to Babylon, Miss Lott's home, gave me an order to get the ring and bring it to him upon my return, as he and his wife were reconciled. So I had a real excuse for calling on Miss Lott. When we had finished preliminaries, I presented my note from Mr. Catterdon. The young lady at once produced the ring, a beautiful and valuable chased gold ring. I received it and with care put it in an inner pocket, intending to deliver it to the owner in at least a couple of weeks. The business transacted, Miss Lott brought in a plate of doughnuts and a pitcher of cider. We were the only participants, strange as it seemed to me; not one of the other members of the family came into the room.

Reader, I should have tried to describe the young lady as an introduction, but now, as then, I was so interested that I was oblivious of all else. Well, Miss Lott was a young lady 15, 16 or 17 years of age. Then, as now, she would not tell her age. She was just five feet tall, weighed just one hundred pounds (as I found out later), had a bright yellow complexion and luxuriant black hair. Well, it was not love at first sight, simply mutual tolerance. After spending a very pleasant afternoon, the young lady at parting said, "Mr. Barnes, you will call again." I knew she wanted me to.

So after two years of hesitation on my part, meditation on her part, acquiescence of grandpa, objections from grandma, mutual consultation, capitulation, then consummation we were married January 1, 1873 by Rev. Edwards, Presbyterian minister, in our own house of five rooms completely furnished. Her sister (Aunt) Maria Lott was bridesmaid and my brother, Peter Barnes, was best man. Thirty-seven relatives and friends were present. She was nineteen and I was twenty-three. It was a cold, clear winter day, all conditions favorable.

December 31, 1874 our first baby came, Peter Arthur. He lived five years and then died of hip trouble resulting from a fall. Oliver Thomas, Mabel Cinderella *(see endnote page 79)* and Harry Grisom were born in Tideoute, Pennsylvania. We moved to Olean on December 18, 1877. Three children were born in Olean, making a total of seven in all. Four have died. Oliver, Mabel and Harry are married. We have nineteen grandchildren and one adopted son. On August 31, 1901 we legally adopted George Collins, then six years old, from the Western New York Society for the Protection of Homeless Children in Randolph, New York. We gave him the name George C. Barnes, and he was with us until enlisting in the World War. He is now living in Denver, Colorado.

On January 1, 1898 we celebrated our 25th wedding anniversary, silver wedding, with over two hundred guests. On January 1, 1923 we celebrated our golden wedding anniversary, fifty years, with over three hundred guests present. Of the thirty-seven present at our marriage, not one was living at our fiftieth anniversary.

We are now entering our fifty-third year of married life. Mrs. Barnes is old, and I am four years older, but we are enjoying excellent health, supported by a lucrative business, and enjoying beyond expression our three children and seventeen (sic) grandchildren.

Before concluding, I must retrospect. My brother remained in the Colored Orphan Asylum for two years after I left. From there he went to Brooklyn and was placed in an apprenticeship of five years under a French chef at Congress Hall in Albany, New York and became a professional. Later he came to me at Great Bend, New York in the chicken business but went back to Albany as a chef. He then returned to Tideoute in the restaurant business. Contracting tuberculosis, he went to Denver's Colorado Springs for his health. Failing, he came home to me in Olean, New York and died in his thirty-eighth year. He never married and always made his home with me.

My Aunt and Uncle, Peter and Caroline Williams, their two daughters both married, went south during the reconstruction period. By bad investments and the Ku Klux Klan, they lost everything and then went to Indianapolis, Indiana. Uncle, old and broken in health, came to live with me a few years in Olean. After his return to Indianapolis, he died after a short illness at the age of eighty-four. My Aunt and her youngest daughter, shortly after his death, came and lived with me for five years. The old lady died, and we sent her remains to Indianapolis for burial beside her husband. The daughter returned after a few months and not a long time after, she also died.

Thus it devolved on me to care for them in their old age as they had for me in my youth. The first fifty dollars that I earned after completing my apprenticeship I gave to my Aunt as a Christmas gift.

In speaking of my Uncle's family, I must make special mention of my cousin Elizabeth, "Lizzie" as we called her. She received a thorough education, and every advantage that money could secure was accorded. Graduating from the Boston Conservatory of Music, she became a cultured musician, a professional pianist. She possessed a rich soprano voice and was an accomplished singer. She took special interest in me, and many a happy hour was spent for my pleasure and entertainment of the family with voice and instrumental music. Many of those old selections are fresh in my memory - "Flee as a Bird to the Mountain," "One Summer's Eve with Pensive Thought," "Sweet Spirit Hear My Prayer", etc. and an endless repertoire of sacred, sentimental and popular music. The following is a newspaper account of her marriage. The envelope filed with the clipping reads: "The enclosed clipping is from the Brooklyn Eagle April 1867 (T. H. Barnes)."

GENERAL CITY NEWS
A Grand Wedding Among the Colored Folks

A very pleasant company assembled last evening at the house of Mr. Peter A Williams, on Putnam Avenue, to celebrate the nuptials of Miss Elizabeth J. Williams and Mr. William Furniss. The Rev. John Peterson officiated, accompanied by four or five other clergymen. The bride was dressed in white satin, with headdress, veil, etc., presenting a magnificent appearance. The company consisted of ladies and gentlemen of intelligence, wealth and worth. The ladies were dressed generally with magnificence, with diamonds and other brilliants, satins and silks; the gentlemen were in full dress with diamonds, white kids, etc. The married couple had presents of gold, silver, and china, the beautiful being judiciously interspersed with the useful, including many articles from friends at a distance. The attendance was from Washington, Baltimore, Philadelphia, Boston and other cities as well as from Brooklyn. Frederick Douglass was expected to be present but did not arrive. The company in the aggregate represented much wealth, individuals being worth sums ranging from $150,000 downward. Prominent were the employers of the groom, two merchants of New York City. After the ceremony came music and dancing and a sumptuous dinner, comprising every delicacy of the season. The company did not separate until a late hour.

After an extended wedding trip to Philadelphia, Baltimore and Washington, William resumed his position with Drake Brothers Bankers and Brokers on Broad Street in New York for about a year. Then he received an appointment as State Librarian of Mississippi at Jackson and Elizabeth was a teacher at the Alcorn State University, making good for a couple of years. They were summarily ordered away in ten days by the Ku Klux Klan. Going to Indianapolis, he accepted a position in the city post office as Superintendent of Special Delivery, a position he held for twenty- eight years. She was a teacher in the public schools. In a contest for superintendent of public schools, she won first place; but again the accursed race prejudice defeated her. Over-study and disappointment wrecked her health, and for over twenty-five years she was an inmate of a hospital where she later died. I visited her after an absence of twenty years. She insisted on going to the piano. We sang and played the old songs, to the delight and entertainment of over one hundred convalescents, nurses and doctors. She was known there as Madam Furniss, musical director, and she died about a year after my visit.

The Furnisses had two sons, now eminent physicians in their respective cities Dr. Harry W. Furniss of Hartford, Connecticut who served in the Diplomatic Service during the Roosevelt administration as minister to Haiti and Brazil and Dr. Sumner A. Furniss, a leading physician of Indianapolis.

Elizabeth's younger sister, Sarah V., received the same exceptional educational advantage; going south with the family, she married the Honorable Samuel Ireland, President of the Alcoin University. She held a position as teacher, efficient and proficient, but the same white specter ended their success. They, too, received an order from that august, imperial organization, the Ku Klux Klan, to leave the state immediately. Ireland, her husband, took sick and died. She went to Indianapolis, and accepted a position as Superintendent of Schools in kindergarten. All went well until a jealous rival informed the Board of Education that Mrs. Ireland was a colored woman. They at once trumped up some technicality and asked for her resignation. Going to St. Louis, Missouri she married an eminent physician of the city, a Dr. Cousins. After a few years of success the doctor died. She returned to Indianapolis and was engaged as a governess, traveling companion and nurse, Sarah Virginia Williams, Mrs. Ireland, cousin of T. H. Barnes.

Health failing, she concluded to come to Olean with her mother. Here she was engaged by the Hamilton Club, their first Matron. After her mother died, she returned to Indianapolis and died there. Theirs is an example of the ever-present race prejudice that balks the colored people's prosperity. Although of gentle birth, endowed with natural tact and energy, possessed of a pleasing attractive personality refined by culture, efficient by education and exceptional accomplishments, yet on the threshold of every success was that black, ignorant specter, Race Prejudice.

I have not been a financial success but perhaps flatter myself in believing that I have been a good provider for those dependent on me. I thank God for robust health. At wide apart periods, I have had critical sicknesses of short duration, but they proved to be a renovating process. I have tried to live a temperate life in all things. Now, at seventy-five, I find myself a poor man but endowed with perfect health, perhaps mentally deranged as this article may prove; we cannot see ourselves as others see us. I owe my well being to God, the giver of all good gifts and graces, to a Christian father and mother of sound mind and body, to an aunt and uncle second only to my parents for their love and care for me, and to the Colored Orphan Asylum Association for the excellent home and Christian example.

"Colored Orphan Asylum" - how correctly named, for we certainly represented every shade of color that amalgamation of the red blood Negro and the blue blood Caucasian could produce, with an occasional distinct trace of American Indian. We were one hundred percent American, for we were direct descendants of the first families of America, on both sides - Jamestown, Virginia 1619 and Plymouth Rock 1620. Our forefathers worked, fought, bled and died in every sanguinary or commercial strife for the uplift and maintenance of this country and government. Our genealogy embraces every American name from Washington to Lincoln inclusive. Patriotism is our motto; no treason, no traitor, no red anarchist. Perhaps our amalgamation will show socialistic tendency.

As varied in color so also were the personal characteristics of the inmates. There were those whose innate courtesy and grace proved them to be of cultured and refined breeding, affable, affectionate, and of natural intelligence. Characters of this description were not few. On the other hand, there were a few who were coarse, brutal, ill-bred degenerates. And as Christ said of Judas, "It would have been better had they never been born." I speak of these types to prove that colored children are not different from others under like conditions of parentage or environment. We sometimes had visitors that came as to a zoo. "Why, these niggers eat the same things we do! And teacher, do they really have names or do you number them? And do you teach them from books?" etc. Such people furnished us with a good laugh. There used to be a great many dense white people.

While in the institution, I contracted the habit of collecting souvenirs, curios, etc., principally from gifts, awards and prizes, books and other articles. Upon leaving, I had quite a collection. Several of them are still in my possession. In Yonkers I received two canes, walking sticks, as presents thus forming a nucleus of a collection of one hundred and thirty-eight now on hand. Every one was a gift, not one that I bought. They represent as many different people; each cane has a history or tradition. I do not prize them for their intrinsic value but the sentiment and friendship they represent of friends and acquaintances. They are as varied as their number. From a rough bow, cut from a tree to the polished ebony, gold head specimen. There is one that belonged to Johnathan Barrows, the first Governor of New Hampshire, one of the signers of the Declaration of Independence; John Brown, the martyr at Harpers Ferry, West Virginia John Jasper of "Sun-do-Move" fame; Bert Williams, the comedian; and from Presidents, Governors, Statesmen and tramps. There are also canes from Africa, Japan, Italy, Germany, Switzerland, England, Scotland, Ireland, Canada, the West Indies, Mexico and just about every state in the Union. It is a pleasure to exhibit the collection since visitors are much interested. I have been requested to "will" them to the "Olean Historical Society Ole Timer's Association."

FRATERNAL

I have been active in fraternal organizations. Several years ago, I was elected an honorary member of G. D. Bayard Post No. 222, Department of New York, Grand Army of the Republic, Olean, N.Y. This distinction I prize highly for there is no organization of men that I revere more than the Grand Army of the Republic, the Boys in Blue of '61. The men who fought, bled and died for the preservation of the Union and with it came the emancipation of four million slaves, making this, in fact, the land of the free and the greatest nation on earth.

I was especially interested in "Bayard Post" from the fact that two of its members were present at the infamous July Riot of '63. L. P. Abott was a member of the first regiment that came to the relief of the city, at the 7th Ave. Arsenal. They quelled the mob by firing "Grape and Canister" (a specific type of machine gun). Hundreds were killed.

L. Y. Miller was an officer on board a gunboat that came into the New York harbor and lay in readiness to bombard the City in case the secession Rebel Riot should gain full possession of the City. Both men just mentioned became my personal friends, and we enjoyed many interesting reminiscent conversations. But alas, taps have sounded. They have answered the bugle call, gone to that camp from whence no solider returns, but in memory they are ever present.

FREDERICK DOUGLASS

One of the greatest Americans of Negro blood whose name is often confounded with that of Stephen A. Douglas (one of the two Democratic candidates for President in 1860 against Abraham Lincoln, Republican) was Frederick Douglass, born a slave. He learned to read and write by force of indomitable will and cunning, copying signboards, bill posters and imitating white school children. He became one of America's greatest orators of his time. Endowed with a wonderful personality, he acquired a culture and intelligence to a wonderful degree. He early espoused the cause of freedom and slavery, thereby suffering all manner of indignities, prosecution and physical abuse, but succeeded in reaching the top in fame. He was heard and applauded by the best in America and Europe that did much to foster public sentiment against slavery and to bring about the ultimate freedom of his people.

Twice I remember he visited the Colored Orphan Asylum. He was a personal friend of my uncle, Peter A. Williams, always visiting the home in Brooklyn when in the city.

I will relate an incident of my acquaintance with "Fred" Douglass. I was an apprentice at the Susquehanna Depot in Pennsylvania. My employer, Samuel T. Johnston, had engaged or secured Douglass to speak in "Nickol's Hall." He got out several hundred large handbills, stating that the famous "Fred" Douglass would speak on a certain date. He sent me out to post and distribute them through the town. I should state that this town was very prejudiced against colored people, would not allow one to remain overnight if known, other than the Johnston family. I started with paste, pail and brush. Soon I was followed by a crowd of boys and men. As I would paste and stick up a bill they would tear them down, stating that they were not going to let any nigger deliver a speech in that town. Their actions attracted attention and wonderfully advertised the event. Johnston became somewhat nervous over the outlook. But several of the good people came to him offering protection, etc. Johnston telegraphed

Douglass to get there on a night train the day before. In so doing, Johnston took him secretly to his home. On the day advertised, every train was visited by a gang of boys and men, declaring that they would not let the nigger light.

The admission was twenty-five cents, and many tickets had been sold to the better class. That evening, when the hall was opened, a great crowd of men forced their way in (would not buy a ticket) armed with potatoes, onions, turnips, sticks and stones. Several white friends with Douglass and Johnston held a consultation at the house, discussing the situation. Douglass was equal to the emergency, having had similar experiences. He suggested that Mr. Young, a white lawyer with Johnston, and himself enter the hall from the rear to the back of the stage. The other men, three or four, were to go to the front to keep peace if possible. So at the appointed time, the hall was crowded to its utmost capacity, no one seated.

Dozens were howling, "Where is the nigger?." Through a door at the back of the stage, Lawyer Young stepped onto the stage, rapped loudly for quiet, and implored the crowd to be silent and that Mr. Douglass would appear. They paid no attention to him but kept howling "Bring out your nigger!" Douglass rushed in talking, pushing Young to one side. Strange as it may seem, the mob quieted at once. They were eager to hear what he had to say. Douglass stood there, the very personification of dignity and composure, a personality that demanded respect, and for an hour and a half held that mob spellbound. Many times he was interrupted with cheers and clapping. When about to conclude his speech, there were cries, "Go on, Go on!" and he did. When finished, several of the gang volunteered to pass their hats for a collection, and over three hundred dollars was placed on the stage. Dozens of men pushed their way to the stage, and Douglass was overwhelmed with rough but complimentary words and acts. He left by the back entrance to evade the crowd. After the speech, the following conversation was heard between two Hibernians in the street. "Pat, that nigger gave us the best speech I ever heard." "Tut, tut, Jimmy, he is only a half nigger." "Well, Pat, if a half nigger can talk like that what would a whole nigger do?"

The next day many called at the barbershop to meet Douglass and complimented Johnston for his pluck. Douglass remained in town two days. Johnston invited a few of his friends to the house for a reception (all white), the best people of the place. There never was a more genial and courteous assembly of ladies and gentlemen. During the evening, Douglass himself, taking a violin, played with the piano for several sets of dances. So I have had the distinction of dancing after Frederick Douglass' own music.

Time passed on. Several years later, I heard him speak at an emancipation celebration at Elmira, New York. He had acquired an international fame.

At his death, the colored people of America lost their greatest man. I was honored to be a member of a committee to build a beautiful and fitting monument to that great man. It now stands in Rochester, where he is buried. The committee consisted of:

John W. Thompson	Thomas H. Barnes
Mrs. R. J. Jeffrey	B. H. Simms
Henry A. Spencer	F. S. Cuningham
R. L. Kent	T. E. Platner
Hon. G. A. Benton	E. R. Spaulding
Hon. H. S. Greenleaf	J. E. Mason
Bishop A. Walters	B. F. Cleggett
T. Thomas Fortune	T. Duffin

On the east side of the shaft is the following inscription in bronze, taken from a speech made by Douglass on the famous Dred Scott decision in 1857:

"I know no soil better adapted to the growth of reform than American soil. I know no country where the conditions for effecting great changes in the settled order of things, for the development of right ideas of liberty and humanity are more favorable than here in the United States."

On the west side is the following extract from a speech on West Indian emancipation, delivered at Canandaigua on August 4, 1857:

"Men do not live by bread alone; so with nations, they are not saved by art, but by honesty; not by the gilded splendors of wealth, but by the hidden treasure of manly virtue; not by the multitudinous gratifications of the flesh, but by the celestial guidance of the spirit."

On the north side are these quotations from the speeches of Douglass:

"The best defense of free American institutions is the hearts of the American people themselves."

"One with God is a majority."

"I know of no rights of race superior to the rights of humanity."

On the south side:

"FREDERICK DOUGLASS"

****

ENDNOTES

"My name is Normal on the Grampton Hills…", page 11

The actual quote is from John Home's tragedy in verse, <u>Douglas</u>, the hero's speech: "My name is Norval; On the Grampian Hills my father feeds his flocks; a frugal swain, whose constant cares were to increase his store and keep his only son, myself, at home." Act ii, scene 1, line 42.

"…Mabel Cinderella…", page 69

Mabel Cinderella Barnes married John Calhoun Crawford of Bath, NY. William Henry Bliss Crawford was the fifth of Mabel and John's eight children that survived to adulthood. William Crawford married Miriam Isabel Wexner of Brooklyn, NY. Fanny Crawford and Douglass Barnes Crawford are their children.